Incomplete Stories: On Loss, Love, and Hope

Ebony Adedayo

AYA
Media and Publishing

Adedayo, Ebony J.
Incomplete Stories: On Love, Loss, and Healing
Includes bibliographical references
1. Black 2. African American 3. Race
4. Family 5. Memory
ISBN: 9798533322737

Dedicated to my mother, Jacqueline Hatch, her siblings—Amos, Hazel, Cynthia, and Larry—
And to our entire family:

May the memories forever serve as a tool for our liberation.

Incomplete Stories

Table of Contents

Incomplete Stories

Preface

I was almost ready to release this book. The cover, with a fabulous picture of myself, was done. The layout was complete. And I had received the final round of edits from my editor. I was ready to go, ready to hit print, and ready to start promoting a work that I first started writing in 2016.

But it just didn't feel ready. I couldn't shake the feeling, no matter how much I tried. The story itself felt done. I didn't need to add anything else to it. There was nothing else that I needed to say at this particular moment in regard to how I was (re)constructing cultural and familial history in order to better understand my grandmother's legacy, the person whom *Incomplete Stories: On Loss, Love, and Hope* was originally centered around.

As I wrestled with what to do, a part of me wanted to include the narratives from my trip to Ghana in 2019. I had already written extensively about this topic and presented a paper at the Association Education Research Association (AERA) conference in 2021 on the impact that (re)turn and (re)membrance have on African American women who are in higher education. Including these narratives, albeit critical, felt like it would detract from the main point of my story—so I dropped the idea.

But then something happened. I got a call from a sister in my church asking me to preach on Sunday, May 30, 2021, for a missionary service. I hadn't preached in a while and at the time felt completely overwhelmed with other obligations including cohosting a conference with my colleagues at school, finishing papers, submitting grades, raising a family, and trying to center my wellness as much as possible in the midst of all of this. A part of me wanted to say no because I felt like I just didn't have the time or capacity. But I felt compelled by the Spirit to say yes.

And I am glad that I did. As I began to prepare, praying and asking God for guidance, the idea of (re)membrance and memorializing the sacred stuck out. I initially thought about the woman in Mark 14 with the alabaster box, and the call from Jesus for us to remember her, but I threw out the idea because it felt that scripture would be more appropriate for the Lenten season, which had just passed. Then I ruminated on Jacob, who later became Israel, thinking about his struggle with an angel of the Lord as described in Genesis 32 of the Old Testament text. These scriptures came to mind because of the repeated injunction throughout sacred scripture for the people of God to remember. But I have long struggled with some of the Abrahamic narratives (Jacob is Abraham's grandson) and their relationship to the justification of colonization as well as enslavement in the United States context.

So I came back to the woman with the alabaster box. I came back to her because in her I found the narrative of a woman, a marginalized woman at that, whom Jesus was calling us to (re)member in the context of the gospel. The more I meditated on this scripture, researching the things that stood out, and writing out what I was being led to articulate, the more it became clear that her story needed to be told. Friday evening, just two days before I was supposed to preach, everything came together, and I went to bed feeling pretty satisfied with the outcome.

Saturday morning, I woke up, quickly checked my email, and immediately started in on the workout routine that I had initiated at the beginning of the year. Mid-workout, I had an aha moment as I thought about *Incomplete Stories* and my sermon. With themes that were so similar, I felt that the sermon would be a perfect addition to the story, sort of a part two or a bonus rather than a continuation of the original manuscript. It made perfect sense! And as soon as I concluded that matter, I finally understood what to do with my writings from my time in Ghana.

What is now before you, and I am so excited about this, is an expanded edition of my original story. Divided into three parts, it contains the story about my grandmother (Incomplete Stories), the journal writings from my time in Ghana (A Black Woman's Journey of (Re)membrance), and the sermon that I delivered on May 30 (Go Back and Get it!). Each part, or story, centers the importance of (re)membering, a critical tool for analyzing our experiences as African-ascended people. Throughout the stories, as you will notice, I use ascendant as opposed to descendant, drawing from Derise Tolliver Atta's (2015) work, "Africentrism: Standing on Its Own Cultural Ground," to suggest that we are rising up from our ancestors and history. My hope is that the resulting form of this book will leave readers more engaged and ready to do the work of (re)membering.

Although my focus is on the experience and history of African-ascended people, I believe that others can use similar processes to make sense of their cultural heritage, because the experiences and history of African-ascended people have global implications that touch every people-group across time. We are not just some special interest or affinity group existing apart from everyone else—after all, the first civilizations were found on the continent and the first peoples originated from the continent. Instead, and I firmly believe this, the liberation of the whole world can and will be found in the liberation of African-ascended people as we fight against the seduction to forget our history and insist on (re)remembering.

Part One
Incomplete Stories: On Loss, Love, and Hope

Introduction

"Whenever an elder dies, a library burns down."
African Proverb

Moments of crisis have a way of unsettling you. These moments not only shake your world, but also cause you to question everything that you once understood to be true about that world. The 2016 presidential election proved to be an unsettling moment for me, only superseded by all of the chaos in 2020, including the coronavirus, the continued violence inflicted on Black bodies, and the shit show surrounding the 2020 presidential election, including the insurrection at the capital on January 6, 2021. Lord God, help us all!

In the face of this unsettled feeling, I couldn't help but ask myself who I was. Who was I becoming? Who did I belong to? I asked myself these questions because, while I intellectually understood structural racism and white supremacy as it was playing out in our nation at every turn, my heart still could not comprehend the depth of hatred that many white people held towards people who look like me. No matter how many books I read, including Frank B. Wilderson III's *Afropessimism* and Derrick Bell's *Faces at the Bottom of the Well*, my heart has never been able to accept that this is just the way it is and the way it has to be.

Though my heart couldn't accept it, I couldn't deny what my eyes saw. Derek Chauvin's knee on George Floyd's neck. White women parading around grocery stores with their underwear on their faces because they didn't want to wear masks. Grown-ass white men throwing a tantrum in my neighborhood grocery store, throwing baskets and cussing people out for the same reason. The mob of people flooding the Capitol building with weapons because they refused to accept the outcome of the election. All white supremacy at its finest.

All of this is emblematic of the hatred for Black people that has always been there, the kind of hatred that white folks were no longer content to stew silently in. Of course, these folks have always been here. Just because they stopped calling us the N-word to our faces didn't mean that they had stopped existing. Instead of wearing white robes, they existed behind their badges, in classrooms, in pulpits, and within so-called progressive spaces that were supposed to be down for the cause. But when push came to shove, the push being the election of President Obama in 2008 and 2012, they were ready to put aside all of the feigned pleasantries to show us who they always were. They were enticed to come out of hiding because of #45's rhetoric, including Birtherism. And they were emboldened to stay there because no one in his party dared to stand up to him. And so, because of him, we saw protections for many marginalized people, including people of color, diminish even as protections for corporations and the one percent grew.

All of this has been hard to watch over these last four years. Hard to watch a blatant white supremacist in the white house say so many things against literally everyone who wasn't a cisgendered white male and get away with it. Hard to watch the protests in Charlottesville in 2017. Hard to watch everything that our ancestors fought for in the Civil Rights Movement be dismantled with just one stroke of the pen. Executive orders! And hard to watch the mockery of the Christian faith, a faith that so many of us hold near and dear to our hearts, even as we question its entanglement with white supremacy over the last five hundred years.

The election of Joe Biden and Kamala Harris has not lessened the feelings of horror and anxiety that we are all collectively carrying in our bodies. Many of us want to get our passports together and get up out of here or take up arms to protect our family from dangers seen and unseen. Our nervous systems are jacked up because we are fighting seemingly everything and nothing all in the same breath. We are not only afraid of the police, but we are also afraid of our white neighbors and what they might do if they do not get their way.

It feels as if we are living out the plot of some dystopian novel, or the New Testament book of Revelations. Is this the end of the world? Or rather, is this the end of the United States? Other countries have experienced these extreme levels of violence and instability, but we hoped against all hope that it wouldn't happen here. We felt that the United States, for all of its horror and degradation, was still too good, still too exceptional to ever fall into the trap that other countries have. We felt that we could never really become Rwanda, or Bosnia, or Honduras, or Libya, or any other number of places that have been marred by corruption and vigilante violence. We felt this way because, in spite of what we have experienced here, we bought into the national propaganda that the United States was still the best place in the world to be. We held our noses thinking about the human rights violations happening across the globe, even as we experienced those same violations within our borders because of white supremacy and heteropatriarchy. Even in our poverty and oppression, we felt superior, not realizing that we were one crisis, one election, one charismatic white guy away from everything turning upside down.

So, in the midst of all of the crazy, I turned back to the questions I posed at the beginning. Who am I? Who am I becoming? To whom do I belong? I turned back to these questions because their answers comprise my own origin story. And I believe origin stories have the power to help us find the resolve to push forward in the midst of great chaos and uncertainty. In these stories, I am not so much looking for the truth as I am looking for how we as a people have come to understand ourselves and make meaning in our fragmented world.

But what happens when those stories are missing? Or when they are simply not accessible for one reason or another, as was the case with me? You see, while I could draw on stories from my faith and cultural communities, I had very few familial stories that I could access. Which was unfortunate, because I needed to know how my people had made it through, time after time, despite the odds, so that I could continue to stand in the face of those same odds today.

For years, I felt hesitant about coming right out and asking for these stories. And that hesitancy, or rather fear, is what kept my mouth shut when I honestly should have spoken up. Another part of me simply felt that I had more time to ask the necessary questions that would allow me to weave together the complex tapestry of our family's story. But when my grandmother developed Alzheimer's disease, I knew that I wouldn't be able to capture that history in the way that I had once hoped.

And so, back in 2016, I started to write these letters to my grandmother, imagining what those stories might have been. I asked questions about our family and constructed narratives based on what I could understand at that time. And I analyzed my own life decisions, from being in ministry to working for the City of Minneapolis, in the context of these narratives. These letters will always be to me a reminder about how I, myself, made it over and a reminder that even when I felt I had little to go on, I always had agency and autonomy to define my own reality.

The original letters have now been updated to reflect the fact that as I finalize this, we are in 2021. I did not write the original letters with the coronavirus in mind (who could have predicted that?), but that has now been our reality since the beginning of 2020. And COVID-19 took so much away from us! Including the ability for me and my family to properly bury my grandmother when she passed away in April 2020. Her passing broke something in me. Even though I knew with my head that I would never be able to communicate with her as I once did, it took her passing for it to register in my heart. Her passing solidified the fact that I would never be able to hear her stories and her testimonies of faith and triumph. But it also deepened the resolve in me to (re)construct, to the best of my ability, the fragmented stories about who I am, who my people are, and where I am going. It is as Cynthia Dillard states in her book, *Learning to (Re)Member the Things We've Learned to Forget,* that in the process of (re)membering, we come to understand who we are as "full human beings, as African people, with appreciation for the spirituality and diversity of our memories and stories" (2012, p. 17).

I take on this work of (re)constructing cultural and familial memory knowing that the process is messy and convoluted in and of itself. In this endeavor, I combine the terms highlighted in Na'im Akbar's (1998) *Know Thy Self* that speak of the importance of deconstruction, reconstruction, and construction in the process of education. Reconstruction,[1] is about rectifying the errors of white supremacist education and making it more culturally relevant for African ascended people. Construction, "seeks to advance the critical growth of knowledge … knowledge must ultimately expand our grasp of the Truth and the identification of untruths" (p. 61). As I reflect back on the narratives in these pages, I see Akbar's framework coming through true and strong, even though I didn't write these narratives with his work in mind. This makes me believe that the process I am taking up here to unearth these stories is not so much technical as it is natural and reflexive.

Akbar's work also applies here because, as the reader will soon see, my journey has involved a fair amount of debunking lies. These are lies that I internalized as a result of attending schools, participating in faith institutions, and working jobs that did not consider the Black and African experience to be a legitimate form of knowledge production. I was miseducated in the worst way! And so, the (re)construction of my cultural and familial memory pushes

---

[1] Note: while Akbar uses reconstruction without parenthesis, I chose to use the "(re)construct" form throughout most of this manuscript because my work most closely follows Dillard's.

back against an understanding of my history through the lens of white supremacy for sure, but also against an uncritical approach to Christianity, my faith expression.

This process is and will be imperfect; the stories will be incomplete. And as I grow wiser and gain more understanding of my reality, I will have to return time and time again to this narrative that I am now (re)constructing, to critique it and fill in the pieces that are missing. And I am okay with that. If the opposite of truth is forgetfulness, as Roxanne Dunbar-Ortiz tells us, we have to ardently practice (re)membering and (re)constructing cultural memory, taking it up as a spiritual discipline of sorts, understanding that we will do it imperfectly. The idea of being able to compose a narrative that is perfect, objective, and free of contextual errors is a Western notion that we have to collectively abandon if we want true healing and liberation. This essay written to my grandmother, in spite of its many imperfections, is my act of liberation.

Incomplete Stories

Chapter I

Dear Granny, I've always loved you. I hope you understand that. Ever since I was a little girl, you were one of my most favorite people in the world. Your smile brought me great delight and your house, at least for an eight year old, was full of treasure waiting to be discovered.

I remember playing in the backyard and on your patio during the afternoons you looked after us while Mom was at work. Not too frequently though; you lived at least twenty-five minutes away. But you were close enough that when we needed you, you were there.

One of the things that I always loved about Christmas was coming to your house for dinner—most likely because your deep red carpets made it seem like Christmas was an all-year affair. And that brought me joy.

But Christmas was also the one time of year that I was guaranteed to see family. It was essentially our family reunion—cousins, aunties, and uncles from all over would gather around your table to eat your collard greens and sweet potato pie. I still haven't mastered your pie recipe, though trust me, I will keep trying.

But more than pie and red carpets, I relished the fellowship of my family, the family that your sprawling dining room table brought together. And I gobbled up the stories that were passed around that table just as fast as I did your pie. Learning about our history helped me weave disparate stories of our family together into one coherent whole. I needed to understand more.

When I started writing back in 2005, I promised you that I would sit down and write our family's story. I needed to understand more about the house that the government tore down so that they could build a freeway. I wanted to find out more about how you got your leg injury; I know that there was a house explosion but am missing the details on how, when, and where. And I needed to know more about our beginnings, our heritage. You were thrilled and excited to share your life with me. Though we never did make any concrete plans; I always assumed there would be time.

Chapter 2

When I first moved from Milwaukee to the Twin Cities, we spoke constantly. We talked about family. My visions and dreams. The guy I was dating. The car I wanted to buy. You were always a source of encouragement, admonishing me to pray and persevere in spite of whatever obstacles I faced.

I have no doubt that our conversations were one of the things that helped me make it through my undergraduate experience. Granny, it was rough. I had no idea, at least back then, that people who professed the name of Christ could be so racist. It was one of the things that threw me off about the school I attended, where I excelled academically but was marginalized socially. After my first year, I was depressed because of how isolated and alone I felt. I am sure I shared the stories with you! But I insisted on staying in Minnesota over the summer because I could not stomach the thought of moving back to Milwaukee.

I filled my time with work as much as I could. And when I wasn't working, I took walks to the Mississippi River, which was very close to campus. And I journaled like it was nobody's business. And I spent way too much time praying, in my own opinion. But it was what I had, and what I had held me together.

Sophomore year, when I lived in an honors dormitory, proved to be just as brutal as freshman year. With few Black people on campus anyway, I was the only Black person in that dorm above the library. Feeling more isolated than before, I moved out of it in the second semester into a room with another Black woman. It was the first and only time I roomed with someone Black until I got married. The experience was night and day compared to all that I had endured before.

I didn't find relief until my junior year, when I finally started to form a community outside of the racist campus by leaving the predominantly white church I was attending to attend a multicultural congregation that was close to campus. And then my first senior year, because you know there were two, I was able to get an apartment on campus. Mom was concerned that I would gain too much weight cooking my own food, while you were worried that I was going to starve. I remember telling you that I was having leftover Chinese food for lunch one day, and you said that you were going to send me money to help me out. I don't know what I was expecting but I was slightly disappointed when I opened the mail and saw only twenty dollars. I am not sure what you wanted me to do with it. Lol.

I could not wait to move off campus during my second and final senior year, the bonus year. And I couldn't wait to invite you and Mister to celebrate with me as I walked across that stage and was finally done with the institution that brought me so much pain.

As I grew older, however, our connection changed. Oh, the factors are many, some of them heartbreaking, but still I reached out. But at some point, you stopped calling of your own volition. You congratulated my husband and I on the birth of our children. And you seemed pleased that I found a full-time job after I graduated from seminary. Other than that, you seemed distant. Gone were the conversations we used to have where we would blab on and on about everything.

And then, gradually, you started to lose yourself to Alzheimer's. I remember when my mom first warned me about it. We were down visiting you and you must have repeated yourself twenty times in the midst of one conversation. It was strange to see you like that! And as the years went on, your condition got worse. Mom and her siblings stepped in to take care of you the best that they knew how. There were some snafus along the way, but we traversed them all and got you to a safe place where all of your needs were provided for. I know you never wanted to go into a nursing home or degenerate to the point that you would need care like this, but trust me, we were honestly trying to do our best.

Chapter 3

They buried your husband in the summer of 2016. Did you feel a piece of you leave your body as they lowered him into the ground? It frustrates me that they didn't even let you know that he was gone. You were his wife for over forty years; you had the right to know.

You had the right to grieve even if the capacity to do it escaped you. They took away your agency.

And so it ends like this. I am sorry. We did not know ourselves. You deserve more than this.

And of course, as soon as the nursing home got wind of it, they wanted to come after your house. Yes, the beautiful house that you and Mister built out in Glendale. Yours was the first house on that block in that suburb. You worked and labored for that house. You nurtured us for so many years in that house. You never wanted that house to leave our family; it was your legacy. But this system has a way of robbing people of the things that they worked their entire lives for, especially when those people are Black, so what recourse did we have? The notion of passing on generational wealth, even when we do everything "right," never seems to materialize for us. We must remember that our inability to produce wealth in this way has nothing to do with a failure on our part; after all, so many thriving Black communities, including our own in Milwaukee, were intentionally destroyed, generation after generation. The bombing of the Black community in Tulsa, Oklahoma, the construction of freeways, the foreclosure crisis—these are only a few examples of how they ripped whatever wealth we did accumulate right out of our hands. Their actions are emblematic of white rage, not just over the existence of Blackness but as Bettina Love (2019) states, rage over the accomplishments of Black people.

More than the house, I was obviously devastated over Mister's passing. He passed away less than a year after you were placed into the nursing home, of a broken heart I am sure, among other things. We had to fight to get you into that home; the attorneys did not initially side with my mother and her siblings regarding the importance of having you in a facility that could provide you adequate care. But as God would have it, you landed in the hospital and the hospital was the one that mandated you get the care that we could not secure on our own. November 2015. It was a hard decision but one we made because we were concerned about your well-being. We did it with that in mind, not thinking about how it might impact your husband, who had been by your side every day for over forty years.

We didn't even know he was ill. We did not even know he passed right away. But his unexpected mortality made me wrestle with your own. I know how life works. And I know the trajectory of Alzheimer's. But I just can't bear the thought of losing you forever. Surely you are immortal and have some secret beans hidden in your stash of belongings at the nursing home. Please take those now so that you can revert back to your younger years; it will give us the opportunity to catch up to the prospect of losing you.

There are so many things I want to ask you. So many things that I want to tell you. If I could get another twenty years with you, I would take it in a heartbeat. But the time for that is no more. Now is the time for me to take what you have given me and try to make sense of it to move forward. Here goes nothing!

Chapter 4

You once told me that your father was a part of the sanitation worker's strike in Memphis—the day before Dr. King was assassinated on April 4, 1968. You said that he was in his fifties at that time and the job had no respect for his age or the length of time that he had been there as younger and more experienced white people came on the job and moved up in position and pay. Of course, the Black workers, your father included, protested.

Besides this fact, I know very little about our family's history of activism. Perhaps, this is because we are so private—we share very little with each other, even the minutest of details are top secret. But maybe you just weren't that involved, as the demands of a young family kept you from engaging at a national level. Maybe you were more focused on the hyperlocal. After all, once you moved to Milwaukee in the sixties, you lost your home to the construction of the freeway. Like so many other Black families that migrated North, there were not many places where we could live. But we found one in Bronzeville, right off of North Avenue. In Bronzeville, Black people made a name for ourselves. We did well for ourselves. And then, just like everything that Black people built, the government came in, dismantled it, and took our family's home and gave you pennies for your loss. When I was a child, I saw the remnants of that once vibrant community, full of Black people who were struggling to get by. After all of these years of government disinvestment, it is now gentrifying. Just like so many other Black communities across this country. I know that must make you boiling-hot mad!

I'd like to believe that it was the struggles of raising a young family that prevented you from getting close to the movement. I'd like to believe this because I know you know that the North wasn't less racist than the South. In 1967, in Milwaukee, WI, riots broke out as a result of ensuing racial tension in the city. Many Black people were injured, some even killed, as police and white residents let it be known that Black people were not welcomed there. That message was sent when the city tore down your home as a result of policies such as the Federal Highway Act, which commissioned the build-out of our nation's freeways and sanctioned the destruction of Black communities in order to achieve the grand ole mission. And it was sent when other policies cut off wealth and employment, housing, and educational opportunities to the city's Black residents. And just to be sure that the message was received, white residents stood angrily waving confederate flags as Black residents tried to cross the city's own version of the <u>Mason-Dixon Line</u> to assert their civil and human rights (McFadden, 2017).

But Milwaukee was only a small reflection of what was happening all over the country, as Black people caught a vision of what could be, and white people, likely seeing that same vision, worried about their own survival. Inasmuch as 1967 was about Black liberation, for others in our population it was about white dominance and power, not just in the South, in the North as well. The North had just as much of a problem with white supremacy. In Minnesota, they call that passive aggressive form of white supremacy "Nice." By they, I mean white people. But we Blacks know better than that.

The thing is, I've never heard you talk about the struggle peculiar to Black folks. But to be honest, I did not hear anyone in our family do so either. I'd like to think that I just wasn't listening but the truth is, we were so attuned to a Christianity devoid of all of Jesus' teachings on justice that we were not listening to the cries of our people, let alone understanding our own reality.

From a young age, both you and Grandpa Hatch took me to church. With him, I attended Greater New Birth and got in trouble for trying to catch the Holy Ghost. With you, it was an Assembly of God Church close to your home in the suburbs. Grandpa's church was distinctly Black—the hats, the shouting, the music and drums—my God those drums! I came home with headaches every Sunday that I attended. But I loved it because there was often food and I got a chance to sing in the children's choir.

Yours was a different kind of church, but I loved it too. There was a distinct children's program at yours, so we didn't have to sit in the sanctuary with the adults the entire length of service. It was in that children's program where I found out about salvation in Jesus Christ and I believed. I confessed faith in that belief on Easter Sunday of 1992, mostly because I misunderstood the preacher. But never mind that, you were proud of me and I was proud of me, too. Nearly thirty years later, I have sorted out that confusion and am still going strong in my faith.

As I grew in my commitment to Christ, I started to express interest in pursuing the ministry as a career. You supported me in this. I quickly learned that pursuing that call took precedence over everything else, even my Blackness. No, you never said that. Other people didn't say that. But the nightmares I kept having told me that I had to choose between my Black identity and my identity in Christ. Those nightmares are what forced me to give up my growing R&B collection, consisting of Mary J. Blige's "What's the 411," TLC's "Crazy.Sexy.Cool," Brandy, Tevin Campbell, Monica, and so many others. Those nightmares frightened me into believing that I was doomed to hell if I entertained anything that did not have a direct link to Jesus. I don't believe that this was your perspective, but the absence of an unapologetic pro-Black analysis from you spoke in ways I didn't even realize.

I irritated both my mother and my father with my reductionist approach to the faith experience. I irritated my father more so because he was a part of the Nation of Islam and didn't so much buy into the "white man's religion." And I irritated my mother because Christianity was seemingly the only lens that I could see out of. "Not everything is about Christianity," I remember her saying, as I took a story she told me out of context and concluded that the reason the main protagonist had such a difficult time was because they were a Christian and were persecuted for their faith. In my eyes, their discrimination had nothing to do with being Black. To be honest, my parents presented me with a realistic understanding of the Black experience that wasn't filtered through a religious worldview—in fact, they both allowed their experiences to help them make sense of who God was and how God was showing up in the world. The thirty-eight-year-old me wishes that I had paid more attention to what they were trying to say, but I know that the twelve-year-old me thought that she was too smart for them. So I didn't.

When the nine parishioners at Emmanuel AME were gunned down during their Bible Study in 2015, Evangelical Christians didn't think it was a matter of discrimination but persecution of the Church. It's like so many Christians don't have the language, much less the prophetic imagination, to name the horrors of racism and white supremacy. To many of them, fighting against racism has nothing to do with Jesus. (I've actually heard people say that because racism isn't in the Bible, that it wasn't important to Jesus. But the Bible also doesn't mention abortion, yet they are ready and willing to stand on that bandwagon!) The thing is, when Black people participate in Christian spaces like these, spaces that fail to recognize the inherent anti-Blackness that pervades our society, we are forced to choose sides, and are forced to identify with the cross rather than the crosses we perpetually carry because of history, because of the color of our skin. We are forced to choose between somebody's standard of biblical values and the realities we face every day because of this skin. Because I wanted to escape hellfire, I fell for that ruse and elevated my faith above my racial identity. Once I understood that Western ways of thinking force us into constraining binaries, I stopped choosing between my various identities and CHOSE to hold all of the frames. Did you know that you could do that, too?

Incomplete Stories

Chapter 5

You once told me what your experience with education was like when you were growing up in Tennessee. As was typical for the time, you noted that the public schools were racially segregated and that the schools Blacks attended were not well funded. In addition, you told me something that I had never read about in any book: Like white schools, Black schools operated nine months out of the twelve-month year. And like white schools, Black schools typically resumed in the late summer months. However, unlike white schools, Black schools closed down for three to six weeks, starting in the month of September when Black students left schools to go pick cotton in the fields.

Sharecropping. While you were too little to participate, the memories of being a daughter of sharecroppers, raised in a community with other sharecroppers, stayed with you. So much so that you decided to create a doll later in life, the Sharecropper's Doll, to tell the story about your experience. You gained some traction with your dolls and were able to go around to a few schools to share your story. But once you got sick, this project was halted. In many ways, I feel like it was your last-ditch effort to explain to us, your family, what it was like to live in the South. To share with us the experiences of racism that you had otherwise kept private for so many years.

A part of me believes that you kept those stories close to your heart in order to protect us. After all, you grew up in the 30s and 40s—there was nothing glorious about that era and most folks with any kind of sense would likely try to forget about all of the horrors associated with living in that time period.

The lynch mobs. Who wants to tell those stories and relive the trauma every time they recall the images of burning flesh? I know I wouldn't. That is why I refuse to watch any type of media that perpetuates harm against Black bodies, including videos that circulate of police killing Black people.

The other part of me believes you kept these stories because you were trying to outrun Blackness, choosing silence and respectability as a means to navigate society. Respectability is what many Black folks have believed was our path to full humanity for some time now. We psyched ourselves into believing that if we were good and upright and saved and disciplined that we would be spared the wrath of whiteness. That if we educated ourselves, got good jobs, owned our homes, worked until our last breath, that we would not be a stain on the nation's consciousness. So that's what we did. We gave respectability our all, believing that even if we lost our dignity, we would at least keep our lives.

But you and I both know that our efforts were futile. Our oppression was never built on the lack of respectability; it was constructed on the commodification of our beautiful ebony bodies. We were stolen away from our ancestral home and brought to a stolen land not because we failed to live up to some societal ideal of what it was to be human, but for profit. So, though we labored and gave it our all, we were still cut down like trees. How much have we as a people sacrificed trying to fit in? How much have we lost trying to suppress the trauma that we have accumulated, not only in our lifetimes, but in the lifetimes of those who came before us?

Sometimes I wonder if the suppression of our history is what caused you to break and succumb to this awfulness of Alzheimer's disease. I know that remembering hurt you, but I am convinced that forgetting cost you more! The unfortunate truth is that we live in a culture where we are routinely seduced into forgetting our identity. Dillard describes this process of seduction as "those irresistible moments when we have been enticed away from ourselves, led away from our duties, and have accepted others' principles or notions of identity and proper conduct as our own" (2012, p. 15). I am convinced that when we spend our whole lives forgetting who we are, we inevitably lose the ability to remember in the end.

Incomplete Stories

Chapter 6

Did you see us marching after they killed our brothers, daughters, and sons? Trayvon Martin, Renisha McBride, Eric Garner, Michael Brown, Tamir Rice, Keisha Jenkins, Tanisha Anderson, Jamar Clark, Alton Sterling, Philando Castile, Korryn Gaines, Thurman Blevins, Ahmaud Arbery, Breonna Taylor, and George Floyd—all strong and free, yet because of their Blackness, they succumbed to the fate of others gone on before.

Did you see us protest their murders? Did you see us shut down the roads and reclaim the very freeways that destroyed our homes and diminished whatever wealth we had? Did you hear us chant and scream, cry and pray, trusting God that another reality beyond this constant trauma was at our fingertips?

Although none of this is new, we didn't grow up seeing the perpetual execution of our kin like this. Social media is to blame, at least in part. Within seconds, the scenes of the latest fill our homes. I watched Philando die. Footage of the last moments of Oscar Grant and Eric Garner are still too accessible. And the videos about Sandra Bland came out in 2019. I refuse to watch them! These images haunt our imaginations and push us to our breaking points where, in rage, we sometimes turn on each other. Meanwhile, so many white folks are enjoying it. They have long reveled in Black death. I have heard the stories of how their ancestors used to gather around having a good ole time while our people were lynched. You can't convince me that seeing our bodies battered and bruised makes them more empathetic to our suffering, not when they used to make sport of it! That is why I tend to cringe in diversity and inclusion trainings that use images of our battered bodies to appeal to white sensibilities.

I only have stories to recall of these things, though I am sure it is not the case for you. But I do remember Rodney King. I was ten when the cops who beat him were acquitted, just as my daughter was ten when Breonna Taylor's murderers were acquitted. History repeats itself! The difference is that, unlike my daughter, I did not grow up being exposed to the constant influx of these visuals. I grew up surrounded by a different kind of trauma on 37th and Lisbon: intra-community violence. It was the 90s and drugs were pervasive in our community, which I am sure was the root of all of the shooting that popped off on our block. It was so bad that Mister put bars on the door after we moved in and we got a big, scary dog who was all bark but no bite. It was so bad that my mom sent us to live with my dad in New York one summer after our house got badly shot up. It was so bad on our block that my youth pastor, who grew up there many years before, never quite slowed down when dropping us off at home after church. He only stopped long enough for my sister and I to get out of the car, and then he sped off.

Over the eight or so years that we lived on Lisbon, the occupant of the house next door sold drugs, no matter who lived there. Undoubtedly, this is where a lot of the violence that we witnessed came from. Although Mom made a point of making friends with the dealers so that they would not target or harm us, it was still hella scary. This, combined with political pundits who blamed the root of the violence on drugs and gangs, as well as the efforts directed at kids to say no to drugs, like McGruff the Crime Dog and the Hang Tough campaign, let some people in our community believe that mass incarceration and police occupation in our communities was justified. The law said the drug dealers and the gang leaders were wrong, so they believed and internalized that law. The thing is, back then, at least in my neighborhood, no one ever asked how the drug dealers and those with guns got access to those things. Michelle Alexander hadn't gotten her research together yet, so we didn't even know that we were asking the wrong kinds of questions.

After spending eight years living in a war zone, we moved up and out—like the Jeffersons. And for the first time in my life, I felt a sense of hope that we could really escape this. Though living on 66th and Villard, where we ended up moving to, was still no Whitefish Bay or even Glendale for that matter, it definitely felt easier to navigate. Mom felt safe enough to let me catch the bus thirty minutes away from our home to go to work and balked a lot less at the idea of me taking the bus at 6:30 a.m. to go to school. That never would have happened on 37th and Lisbon.

Funny thing is, in spite of all of the trauma and chaos in that neighborhood, I feel a sense of nostalgia when I think about it. I attribute this to the fact that it was where I came of age and where I began to develop a sense of identity. It was also where I fell in love with my culture (you know, before the whole white supremacist approach to Christianity). It was where I was exposed to West African dance by taking dance lessons at a community center on the East side. My dad played the drums for them, which I thought was the coolest thing. (I still think he is the baddest drummer there is.) We also, on occasion, celebrated Kwanzaa in that house. Though

I did not know its meaning back then, it felt cool to have a holiday that we could celebrate right after Christmas. I was first exposed to Arrested Development, the Winans, Anita Baker, Kris Kross, Whitney Houston, Janet Jackson, and so many others in that house. I watched their videos on "The Box" and tried to master Janet Jackson's moves from "Rhythm Nation." She and Whitney Houston were my idols!

I say all of this to say that, despite what we went through, the violence, the shootings, and so many other things that I dare not mention in this essay, I loved being there. I was glad to move when we did; I needed a freedom as a teenager that that house wouldn't afford. But I never dream about our house on Villard. I seldom think about the time that I spent there. Perhaps it's because I only lived there three years before I moved to Minnesota for school. But perhaps, it's because the things that meant so much to me on Lisbon, my culture, didn't matter to me as much when I lived on Villard.

If I am honest, Granny, a part of me equated my own personal liberation to the liberation of my people. Or at least, when I didn't have to come face-to-face with the hopelessness, I forgot about it. Again, this is not to say that Villard was paradise (we were only on the other side of the Westlawn projects), it is to say that we all, you included, began to breathe a little easier when we left Lisbon.

Sometime in my youth, I turned my attention to the needs of the world. I am pretty sure this newfound passion had everything to do with the missionaries and evangelists who regularly visited our multicultural church. I was inspired by their witness and felt that if I was going to honor my faith, I should be like them.

I took my first missions trip two years after we moved to the house on Villard. I went to El Salvador for two weeks with a team of about twelve or so people. Though it was not my first time out of the country (I went to Canada when I was in seventh grade), it was my first time to a place that didn't speak English as a primary language. This, in addition to the sights, the smells, and the customs, frightened me even though my Spanish-speaking ability was pretty good. Not fluent good. But good enough. The first few days that we were there, I had this conversation with God because I was just too uncomfortable with the whole thing. I wanted to leave. So I asked God to help me adjust. And I believe He did, which is good because there wasn't any way I could leave anyway. And when I returned home, after two weeks of being away, I stood at the bus stop in front of the house on Villard, asking God what my purpose was in the United States because I was too unsettled. I found more value in a foreign land telling somebody I didn't know about Jesus. I always thought that it was my calling. But perhaps, maybe my body knew then what I can clearly articulate now; the United States is and will always be inhospitable to Black folks. Perhaps this was why I was so unsettled coming back.

Unable to distinguish between a sense of purpose and my body simply wanting to get the hell up out of dodge, I went on my second missions trip after my senior year in high school. While this experience was impactful, I also felt marginalized in a way that it took me decades to understand. I didn't know then what I know now about how racist the Assemblies of God was! And this was the denomination that sponsored the missions trips that I participated in. While individual pastors were fine, after all I liked all of the pastors in my home church in Milwaukee and even the pastors in the church I spent a significant amount of time in Minneapolis, it seemed like as a whole, the denomination was either promoting or producing clergy, and congregants for that matter, who were not only disconnected from the Black experience but had absolutely no desire to build meaningful, nonpatronizing relationships with us. As a result, I spent most of my time in Argentina in tears, trying to figure out why the lead pastor on that trip despised me so. It was something about his tone and his treatment towards me that set off all of my alarms.

Because I couldn't understand my experience or what my body was trying to tell me, I went off to college to pursue missions studies. You were so proud of me. I carried that pride as boldly as I could, but you could not have imagined all of the things I went through just to make it through that institution.

I was thinking about that house on Lisbon the other day, just like I often do. Something prompted me to look it up on Zillow to see if it was up for sale. If it was, I honestly would have considered buying it. It is so cheap. Because again, the neighborhood (and because housing prices in Milwaukee are considerably lower than they are in the Twin Cities). It wasn't though. So I looked at the house on Villard, not because I wanted to buy it but because I was curious. And then, finally, I looked up your home on Longview in Glendale. I wasn't ready for what I saw. They completely remodeled it, Granny. Gone are your red carpets and those beautiful cushions that matched it. Gone are your initials above the fireplace. Gone is every semblance of your presence over these last several decades. They erased your essence and the history of that place, minimized the fact that in the midst of a sea of whiteness, a Black family existed and remained steadfast all of this time. Your existence was your protest, your protest against a city that once ripped your house right out from under your family. And now it is gone. Just like the home in Bronzeville. I don't care about the shiny new marble and the island that they put in the middle of the kitchen. I just want it back the way it was! White supremacy is a B&%^$.

Chapter 7

I did the missions thing for a while, or at least, I accumulated nearly a hundred thousand in debt so that I could pursue it. I just knew that the world was where God was calling me; the US didn't have any issues that needed to be solved in my little imagination. I remember a friend of mine from the Caribbean asking me why I did not exhibit the same commitment towards my own. I still shudder at my reply. Truth was, I was blinded to the plight of my own people because my Western faith expression did not have a place for it. I continued to interpret every single life experience through the lens of Western Christianity, a lens that did not validate or even try to explain the experience of people who had been systematically oppressed.

It did not take me long to come to my senses. Life has a way of putting you in your place, whether you like it or not. And as reality looked me dead in my face, I yielded to the Holy Spirit and began the process of coming to grips with who I really was—a dark-skinned Black woman living in one of the most racist countries on earth.

Yet, my identity as a Black woman stood in stark contrast to the form of Christianity that I was taught to embrace. But the more I read the scriptures, the more I saw myself and my experience reflected in them in a way that I had not picked up on before. Gone was the over-spiritualization of passages that were calling out structural oppression and exploitation. I began to see this ancient text, the Bible, for what it really was: a testimony of God's faithfulness to the exploited people of the world.

The moment I understood that God was deeply concerned about exploited folks like me, and moreover, that God was concerned about Black women, it gave me the permission to look for our stories wherever I could find them. I started paying more attention to womanist theologians like emilie townes and Delores Williams for more of a Black feminist approach to the world and to the Word. I took up Alice Walker, Zora Neale Hurston, bell hooks, Toni Morrison, Cynthia Dillard, among others, not just as intellectuals, but spiritual guides who were gifting me the language I needed to articulate my situation. Though I was mad as hell for not being able to access them earlier in my life journey, I was grateful to look into the faces of these fierce Black women as they poured out knowledge from the depths of their soul just so that I could find salvation.

My priorities began to shift. I wanted to still serve in a church, but only if the congregation was committed to racial justice and anti-oppressive work. That commitment caused me to leave a church that I attended for nearly ten years in search of something more aligned with my passion for justice. The first place where my family and I landed was out in the suburbs. The pastor talked a good game that tickled my ears at first. But that was all it was, game, so we left after eighteen months. Quite honestly, I checked out around month fifteen or sixteen when he declared that "the South would rise again" from the pulpit. Though there were apologies for what he understood to be an expression and appreciation of culture, and not, you know, white supremacist commitment to Confederate ideologies, I never took that church seriously after that.

We left for another church that actually seemed as if it was doing anti-racist work. Because of my commitment to ministry, I decided to intern there, while working a full-time job and raising two very small children. A friend of mine asked me how many internships I needed since I had completed my master's degree four years prior and was already more than qualified. I knew what she was getting at with her question but also felt that I was in a place where I had to always prove my expertise to be accepted anywhere.

This is a Black woman's burden. I understood that. I understood that a white man with little college education would be more acceptable in the pulpit than me with two degrees behind my very Black-sounding name. Yes, it infuriated me and yet, I knew of no other way. At least, I knew of no other way inside of the institutional church. So, I became intent on creating opportunities outside of it, not because I stopped believing in Jesus, but because I started believing in me.

Incomplete Stories

Chapter 8

One of the most important things I have learned over the years is the notion of structural racism and oppression. I used to believe that racism solely functioned at an individual level, and my imagination mostly pictured dudes in white robes burning crosses or some bigot shouting the N-word. These were obvious forms of racism that most folks in all of their naivety cannot deny.

But the idea of structural oppression, or that racism was codified in a system of laws and practices in the United States, was new to me. It took me a while to understand the depths of that. Honestly, I think my Western ideas of individualism and Christianity got in the way. Or perhaps it was because, even without the burning crosses and hoods, I still saw far too many racists walking around, hiding behind the veneer of Minnesota-Nice progressivism. Their passive aggressive behavior made it impossible for me to abandon the idea that structural racism was our only foe—structural racism has and continues to be nurtured by individual attitudes, practices, and behaviors. The realtors who refuse to sell homes to Black families are acting out of individual prejudices that then get formulated into de facto laws. And employers who refuse to hire Blacks—regardless of education and experience—are acting on their own biases in spite of the mandated equity and inclusion workforce goals. The attitudes of the most bigoted and powerful among us get baked into laws that govern Black bodies and dictate when and where we walk, live, worship, and play.

Then there is this thing called White Fragility. Granny, I try to be careful with that terminology because I think it lets white people off the hook far too easily. They ain't fragile! Yet, I do understand that the way that they have been socially conditioned renders them mostly incapable of dealing with racism and the gravity of the harm that they have done to the Black body since at least 1607. Because of their inability to process and address harm, our very presence threatens their identity.

I know that some of this has to do with the fact that they didn't expect us to make it this long. We've survived the brutal crossing of the Atlantic, slavery and rape, the convict-leasing system, Jim Crow, mass incarceration, and in spite of what it seems, police brutality cannot kill all of us! Darwin and his comrades thought that we would just die out, thinking that we were so genetically inferior. But in 2019, we celebrated more than four hundred years of being on this soil and guess what, WE ARE STILL HERE! Maybe they didn't think we would be this resilient, this steadfast in the face of the ever-morphing racist attacks against us. And maybe this ongoing existence is a residual reminder of what they did to us (which is why Lincoln wanted to send us back to Africa after emancipation rather than allow us to be free on this soil). As much as they strike us from their history books, forget our names and contributions, and sanitize our prophets, our presence is a constant reminder of their oppression against humanity. They were the criminals, the soulless bearers of inextricable evil against Divine-image bearers, forsaking their own identity for the sake of whiteness.

Whiteness comes at a great cost, not just for Black people, but for white people too. They have had to give up their culture, their language, their land, and their innate ways of doing things for the sake of this American idea. It has left them devoid of understanding and of identity. And so the only thing that many of them can place their identity on is this sense of superiority over us Black people. Even when that superiority does not actually yield anything to them at the end of the day, they will go to great lengths to protect their sacred myths. And they will go through hell and back to defend the so-called American Dream, a dream that in fact proves to be a nightmare for them to the extent that many in their community are suffering exponentially. The pastor in me wanted to reach out, wanted to solve their crisis, wanted to be their Black savior. For many years, I did that, thinking that if I uttered the right magic words from the pulpit that they would repent of their ways and surrender their racism. I felt that this work was my divine call. But 2016 woke me the hell up from this delusion, and the work of people like Ta-Nehisi Coates in *Between the World in Me*, began to free me from this obligation to save white people and help them get woke. "Do not struggle for the Dreamers. Hope for them. Pray for them, if you are so moved. But do not pin your struggle on their conversion" (Coates, 2015 p. 151).

I thank God for these words. These words set me free from the desire to save white people at my own expense. Because of these words, I quickly grew tired of falling on my own sword for their salvation, knowing that no amount of Black death is capable of atoning for their sins. We cannot be their saviors; they must rescue themselves!

Incomplete Stories

Chapter 9

I think the biggest identity crisis for white folks are our nation's changing demographics. In less than twenty-five years, our country is slated to have more people of color and people who are indigenous to what is now considered the United States than white people. Even now, there are more children of color being born than white children. Which is exciting to me at least!

But the same thing that fills me with joy is a source of anxiety for white people because they fear loss of wealth and power amidst the changes. The election in 2008 put a face to many of their fears as a Black man from the southside of Chicago, who was reared by a single mother (he embodied all of the stereotypes!), was elected to one of the highest seats of power in the world. Obama's election sent shock waves down the spine of white people who saw his administration as a threat to their well-being. From the moment he secured his seat, they gave him nothing but trouble. I am sure you took notice as the Tea Partiers hoisted themselves into power, seeking to hold on to whatever they could grasp from a yesterday that was quickly fleeing. For all of their disdain towards organizing, they sure as hell did a fine job growing and organizing a base of people who worked to ensure that there would never be another Obama.

In 2010, they unseated many Democrats and moderate Republicans with their rhetoric. But as 2012 came to a close, it was clear that the Tea Partiers had become irrelevant. Though many of those elected held onto their seats, the Tea Party as an organized identity failed to thrive and died a quiet, unsuspecting death.

And in 2015, #45 resurrected pieces of it. The idea of taking the country back, along with his entertaining presence, pushed him into the limelight. Surely, someone of his station—with his toddler-like tantrums and adolescent antics—would be disqualified. God, we hoped and prayed that it would. But the media fanned the flames of his existence and his supporters thought those flames to be true fire. They, overwhelmingly white and anxious over the browning of America, swallowed his words whole, blind to the fact that his rhetoric was as void of nourishment as it is virulent.

I'm not suggesting that I was with Hillary. She was shady as hell. Hello crime bill! But she was stable. He, on the other hand, re-awakened the consciousness of white folks who feel that they are losing ground in this country that they do not have legitimate rights to. They "earned it" by conquest, genocide, and war, and that is the only way they imagine they can hold on to it. This was essentially at the root of the push to build the Dakota Access Pipeline and the way that those in power responded to the water protectors' agency. And the irony around the rhetoric about Mexicans crossing the border undocumented when the Mexican-American War actually made the border cross them! How they fight against Islam and LGBTQ and women and everyone who is not a cisgendered heterosexual white man! It reminds me of the oft-quoted saying, "If you have a problem with everyone, maybe you're the problem."

The reality is that they are losing ground. Fast. They know it and are grasping to hold on to it by any means necessary. And this is what shakes me to my very core. As a spiritually sensitive person who is well-versed in the Word of God and history itself, I see a change coming. But I suspect that change will not be good for people who look anything like us unless God intervenes.

I know you know this! You survived the Great Depression, you lived through Jim Crow, and you witnessed the Civil Rights Movement—you know what they do to us when they fear loss of power and resources. You have witnessed with your own eyes the frequency with which we become the sacrificial lamb for this country's sin, called to atone for that which continues to oppress and marginalize us.

And yet, you are also well acquainted with hope in spite of the permanence of this beast. For you, that hope was rooted in your faith in Jesus Christ and the promise of the Second Coming, where He would come and make all things new. It is this same faith that you passed down to me and that centers me when I would rather cower in fear of the future. In spite of what I see in this present hour, I know that this system of dehumanization and destruction will not last forever because God will pull the veil down on this whole thing. In that moment, we will discover that racism is nothing more than a cowardly wizard hiding behind a twisted version of reality. And God will defeat that wizard, liberating all those who have been oppressed by its grasp. This is the only thing I can cling to! Because without God, I honestly have no hope in this country getting better. I am no fool and won't be gaslit into believing otherwise.

Incomplete Stories

Chapter 10

The day after the 2016 election, I started working for the City of Minneapolis. I started work there believing that I could play a role in reducing the harm Black people were experiencing because of ongoing police violence. I started working there months after Ashton Sterling, Philando Castile, Korryn Gaines, and Sylville Smith were killed by police officers for being Black.

I believed I could make a difference because I was committed to the well-being of our people. I felt like that commitment was enough to work inside of a government system. And even if I could not make a difference in the way that I hoped, I believed that I could at the very least get the community valuable resources related to mental health and wellness.

I was wrong. Sure, I mean, my presence has probably helped to a degree that I can't quite recognize at the moment. Only God knows. And only time will tell as, years down the line, people draw on the capacity-building opportunities that we made available. Over the years, this hope in the long-term community benefit has been central to my work and how I have done it, including the way that financial resources are given out to organizations to do work, the way that programs and initiatives are constructed, and the reasons why those initiatives are constructed in the first place. The relationships that I have built over the years as a result of this work have brought me immense joy. But the joy is easily overshadowed by the intense level of harm that I have endured as a result of working for a system that routinely kills Black bodies.

All institutions are racist. We know this. All institutions have a way of silencing Black people, in particular Black women and trans/gender-nonconforming people. All institutions have a way of minimizing our contributions, even as they extract more of our time, energy, and intellectual capacity. But there is something to be said about working for an institution, like city government, that actually kills Black folks. No other institution, outside of the armed forces perhaps, has this capability. And this is why the harm to Black people inside of these places is unique and particular to those who share the same experience.

Since I have worked for the city, there have been countless police killings. Before the murder of George Floyd in 2020, the only officer who was held accountable for his offenses was Somali.[2] Everyone else has gotten away with murder, and as staff, we have not been able to talk about it. When I first started working for the city, someone told me that I had to be careful about how I discussed these issues because the police were my coworkers. My colleagues within the department where I worked, in essence, became one of my only outlets, the only safe space to discuss what was happening to me without being reprimanded. I was already bumping my head against the wall hard because of the way that I centered community needs in my work, as opposed to centering the institution. Again, I was never interested in

---

[2] This manuscript was originally written prior to the conviction of Derek Chauvin for murdering George Floyd. While we rejoice in Chauvin's conviction, the reality is that it took so much evidence to convict him, that it suggests the structure that allows cops to get away with murder has not changed and that Chauvin may be an exception to the rule of white supremacist policing.

protecting the system; my commitment has always been about making things better for Black folks.

That is one of the reasons why I took on the 400 Year Commemoration work in 2019, honoring the history of African Americans in this country. This was work that I prayed about for years, long before I even knew that I would be working for the city. In putting together a framework for this commemoration, I planned activities for both Black residents and Black employees of the city of Minneapolis.

One of the activities for city employees focused on having separate spaces for Black and white staff to talk about this history. As soon my colleagues and I launched that work, however, we were attacked on all sides for not pursuing our racial justice work in palatable ways for white people. But we refused to stay silent. All of the gloves came off when they tried to throw us under the bus for wanting to protect Black staff and, furthermore, when they did not protect us in the press. The Washington Post, the Minneapolis Star Tribune, and several right-wing publications accused us of being separatist for centering Blackness. The audacity of it all!

The thing is, no one asked us for our thoughts on our own work. No one asked us to explain. No one called us for comments. Their failure to ask had nothing to do with us not being available, but everything to do with taking our agency and suppressing our voice. Luckily, there was this thing called Facebook. And so, since they all refused to tell our story, I took to my own social media networks to tell my story for myself. Because narratives matter! And the storyteller matters. And I, for one, had grown tired of so-called well-intentioned white liberals taking away our mics when we are perfectly able to speak for ourselves.

Nearly a year to the day when city leadership came after us for wanting to hold these sacred spaces for Black and white staff, they murdered George Floyd. While former officer Derek Chauvin was the only one with his knee on Floyd's neck, I say they because the institution has allowed this level of brutality to continue year after year after year. And it hurts.

But the body can only endure so much harm before it either implodes or explodes. My own history of trauma taught me that imploding was not an option (and I am not the exploding type). So I had to find a different way to tell the story about what was happening to me. I talked about it with my therapist. I brought it up in my relationships. I wrote about it as much as I could, hence this letter. I even set boundaries around certain individuals who I believed would exploit my story for their own gain and cause more harm for myself and my colleagues in the end (harm that still happened in spite of those boundaries that my colleagues and I set).

To make matters worse, it felt as if we were not only being ignored—in terms of the level of harm AND the strategies to mitigate the harm being felt by staff and community—it also felt as if we were being forced to put out a strategy to keep the system from crumbling. Even though we had no institutional authority, it felt as if we were being looked to save the same institution that was harming us. Although it felt as if they tried to make us martyrs and mammies simultaneously, we pushed back and kept setting boundaries around what we would and wouldn't do.

I wish the pain stopped there, but it doesn't. Just three months after Minneapolis officers killed George Floyd, Kenosha's police department shot Jacob Blake seven times in his back in front of his kids. It is only by the grace of God that he survived his encounter with the police, as so many don't, yet he is paralyzed from the waist down. Yet, we were all still processing what happened to George Floyd in Minneapolis and around the world, so there were protests to continue to demand police accountability and radical change. In Kenosha, several nights after Jacob Blake was shot, a white supremacist shot and killed two protesters, and wounded another. The very next day, the City of Minneapolis's police department posted a video of a Black man committing suicide, just to prove that they were not involved in his death. It was all too much. It seemed as if I couldn't regulate myself fast enough before another traumatic incident occurred.

And that's just the thing: How much more Black death do we have to witness? How many more images of Black folks being brutalized must we give account for? The catch twenty-two is that if those images are not there, we do not have visuals to testify against the system. But we still don't get justice even when the images are there and the evidence is as clear as day.

I imagine none of this is new to you. You've been through this before. You lived in the South. Hell, you lived in Milwaukee. You know this country's sick fascination with the lynching of Black people—whether by a cop, a vigilante, or someone taking their own life. You know how these people have made a sport out of our suffering, even as they spout rhetoric to make us believe that they are truly committed to transformation. You lived for eighty-eight years and never saw justice on this land. How much more do we have to endure as a people before we can see it? Will we ever get it here?

Chapter 11

Here's the conundrum that most of us don't like to talk about: As difficult as it is to explain racism and convince people to fight for racial justice, it is much more challenging to convince people to fight on behalf of Black women. It is more challenging to convince people to fight for us because many believe that the intersection of white supremacy and patriarchy is just an illusion, a derivative of white feminism, and a distraction. But none of these things are true.

Many people readily ignore our cries for help and minimize our contributions, as if our work is not meaningful—even as they try to take credit for it and capitalize on it. I experience this lack of regard, compassion, and respect from white people all of the time. From white men who thought that they could have access to my body. From white women who scoffed at the idea that others could find a Black woman like me sexually appealing. From the white woman who decided to go on Facebook to announce that the reason Black women could not get a Black man was because we were too angry, too aggressive, too Black. From whites of both sexes who had ideas about how I should show up professionally and who reprimanded me when my voice was anything but affirmative of theirs. From white-adjacent folks, who, either because of the lightness of their skin color, pedigree, or access to power, felt that they could be down for racial justice in public, only to step on me and other Black women in private.

When Black women start to point out microaggressions like these, very few people take our complaints seriously. They don't take it seriously because historically, the harm that

Black women endure in this country has never been taken seriously. The myth of the Strong Black Woman is so readily attached to us because it is believed that we can endure more pain, more disappointment, and more heartache than anyone else, and still show up in empowering ways for everyone else.

Here's the thing, and this is really hard for me to say. The harm that Black women experience doesn't just come from white folks and other people of color. It sometimes comes from those closest to us, our Black men. To be clear, I am not saying all Black men are out here harming Black women. I know plenty of them who don't. But what I am saying is that the system of patriarchy privileges Black men in such a way that unless one is conscious and actively resisting it, they can still hoard power and dominance over Black women. I've seen this kind of harm play out in our churches and other faith-based institutions. I've seen this harm play out in nonprofits, the academy, government, business, and in the private domain. This harm is displayed in the shows that we watch and the media we consume. It is also enacted in the failure to protect, advocate, and assume the best of intentions about Black women.

I believe that the root of this problem is the failure of our society to recognize the agency, the humanity, and the limitations of Black women, in the same way that others' agency, humanity, and limitations are honored and respected. This is, in essence, because Black women don't get to be fully human. After all, the slave enterprise was essentially designed around the dehumanization and exploitation of the Black woman's body, for not only labor but for mass reproduction. I've heard it said that nearly every

Black woman who endured the Maafa were raped. And Black women were violated and raped on the plantation to produce more offspring who would uphold the system of slavery after the slave trade was officially outlawed in 1808 (though we know, they didn't really stop until 1859). In spite of the horrors they endured, folks like William Wells Brown (a well-known abolitionist, Granny), accused Black women of having "no greater aspiration than that of becoming the finely dressed mistress of some white man" (Giddings, 1984, p. 61). Comments like his echo the rhetoric of white supremacists, who blamed us for the brutality that we faced, in order to justify what they did to our bodies.

I know I might catch some heat for these words. Some might accuse me of trying to be divisive. Others might accuse me of trying to bring Black men down. None of these are my aim. My point is to shed light on the full extent of what Black women go through. My point is that, as much as we push against white supremacy, we also have to deal with the power imbalance and how power is used against Black women within our own communities. I want to really emphasize power here because while Black women can and do treat Black men horribly, Black men still hold more power over us—both in private and public spaces. Yes, we have agency, and we exercise that agency every single day. But individual agency does not negate the weight of what I am talking about here. And individual agency, unfortunately, does not curb the rates of domestic violence that Black women endure. An article published by the Blackburn Center in 2020 sheds light on the severity of this, stating that Black women are more likely to be murdered by men that white women, by a current or former partner, who is more than likely also a Black man.

Several months before this article was written by the Blackburn Center, I took note of alarming incidents in both Milwaukee and the Twin Cities that unfortunately proved how true these statistics were. And it broke my heart. It broke my heart that these things kept happening and it broke my heart that no one seemed to care about the names of Black women who made it into the headlines because they were killed by their partners. Reflecting on this, I wrote:

> You know
> It wasn't your fault
> You did absolutely nothing to bring on the violence
> leveled against your body
> It wasn't anything you said
> How you looked
> Or how you acted
> But you feel like it was, so you adjust
> You take back the boundaries you tried to set
> You reassure them you are okay even though you are
> boiling on the inside and bleeding on the out
> You go along to get along, attempting to smooth
> things over so that the violence doesn't happen again
> Or so it doesn't get worse
>
> You coddle
> You protect
> But it is eating away at you
> And you are sacrificing your sense of well-being
> because you are too afraid of what lies on the other
> side of the *what-ifs*
> On the other side of this intense pain if you lean into

> it; Instead of pretending it doesn't exist
> *"How Long," Excerpted from* The Gospel According to
> a Black Woman *(Adedayo, 2020, p. 65)*

The Civil Rights Movement of your generation only had the capacity to pay attention to racism. Or at least, this is what many leaders said they only had the capacity to pay attention to. Black women who were looking for rights back then were admonished to put race first, under the notion that if the race as a whole does better, Black women also do better. But so many Black women in the movement were sacrificed at the altar of that analysis. In her essay, "Learning from the 60s," Audre Lorde (1984) confesses that at many times during movement work in the 60s, she felt forced to choose between different aspects of her identity in order for her Blackness to be legible.

Yet, Malcolm X himself said that the most disrespected and unprotected person in America is the Black woman (the Honorable Louis Farrakhan expressed similar sentiments recently). I do not know how his analysis factored into his politics and advocacy. I have not seen any evidence to believe that it did, but I am happy to be proven wrong. However, our movements today are far more intersectional, giving us space to take up multiple positions and multiple identities, so that no segment of the Black community is left behind as we secure our freedom. Author Barbara Ransby (2018) affirms this in speaking to the work of the Black Lives Matter Movement, stating that "this movement has ... patently rejected the hierarchical hetero-patriarchal politics of respectability... emphasizing the needs of the most marginal and often-maligned sectors of the Black community" (p. 3).

One of the things that I believe I have learned from you is to not take no for an answer. In the face of white supremacist patriarchy, you created opportunities for yourself, your family, and so many others. I believe this spirit to create from nothing is found within so many other Black women, Black women who refuse to allow their circumstances to define themselves but who instead, take what they have at their disposal to fulfill their God-ordained purpose. In the end, it may never look like what we initially envisioned; oftentimes the outcome is greater than our hearts could have ever conceived. This reality continues to give me hope, understanding that because of Black women, God is always making a way out of no way.

Chapter 12

Am I a feminist? Yes, I am a feminist in the sense that I wholeheartedly believe (and fight for) the rights of all women. But I also believe that the word "feminism" is too limiting to encompass my entire beliefs.

I prefer Alice Walker's term, womanist. Yes, the woman who wrote *The Color Purple*. In 1983, the year I was born, she wrote this beautiful book, *In Search of Our Mother's Garden*, with the most brilliant essays that articulated her stance and place in the world. In that book, she defined the concept of womanism, to describe what it is to be a Black woman in this world fully exercising her God-given agency: Responsible. In charge. A woman who loves other women. Sometimes loves other men. Committed to the survival of Black people. Loves the Spirit. Loves herself.

I cling to Walker's definition because it is more comprehensive for me. I appreciate that Walker emphasizes the importance of everybody within the Black community moving forward. Black men. Black women. And if she was writing this today, I am sure she would also include Black trans/gender-nonconforming folks too. And children (she misses that, not sure why). This is an important premise for me, because as much as I critique patriarchy, I am not for tearing down, minimizing, moving aside, or doing without our Black kings. Yes, there are serious issues that must be addressed urgently! But my commitment is to addressing and healing the issues, rather than discarding people. I believe that for us to move forward, we have to all move forward together. For me, this means that if we must bump heads along the way to gain a better sense of each other, then that is the work that we must do.

I also appreciate Walker's definition because in it I see her commitment to the advancement of all Black women, rather than individual Black women. Unlike common understandings of feminism, her definition doesn't allow anyone to get thrown under the bus for the sake of political gain. This wasn't the case for white feminists like Susan B. Anthony or Elizabeth Cady Stanton, who were willing to sacrifice Black women at the altar of the Suffrage Movement. They didn't care about Black women and only used them to advance their cause, going so far as to attack Black men who had been granted the right to vote before them. In her book, *When and Where I Enter*, Paula Giddings (1984) speaks to this dynamic, stating that Anthony and Stanton equated giving Black men the right to vote to dethroning "FIFTEEN MILLION WHITE WOMEN—their own mothers and sisters, their own wives and daughters—and cast them under the heel of the lowest orders of manhood" (p. 66). Anthony and Stanton also went to great lengths to minimize the intellectual capacity of Black men in the name of advocating for Black women, concluding that "it would be better to be the slave of an educated white man than of an ignorant Black one" (p. 65). Fortunately, Black women like Frances Ellen Harper saw right through the ruse and said that the greatest obstacle to Black women advancing was not Black men but racism, including that of white feminists. She recognized that just because they shared the same struggles of sexism with Black women, that white women did not automatically make dependable allies. Harper understood what it has taken us far too long to come to grips with: "Being black means that every white, including every white working-class woman, can discriminate against you" (p. 68).

The more things change, the more they stay the same! While the dynamics were different, white women voted en masse for #45 in the 2016 election, in spite of all of the hateful rhetoric that he directed towards them. And the same thing happened in 2020 and will also be the case in 2024 unless white women get knocked over the head by some divine act of God. I don't get it. And I never will. But one thing I do know: In spite of all of their verbiage, most white women have more affinity for their race than they do their gender. Meaning that at the end of the day, no matter how much they say differently, they may sell me out in order to uphold the structure of white supremacy. It is not only history that tells me I should expect nothing different; my own personal experiences also prove that is the case! I have SO MANY STORIES here. But that is for a different day. And a different book.

In addition to Walker's definition of womanism, I appreciate Dillard's (2016) definition of endarkened feminist epistemology, which "articulates how reality is known when based in the historical roots of global Black feminist thought" (p. 407). For me, Dillard really roots this idea of feminism in who we are as African ascendants, and the wisdom, spirituality, and culture that comes from our ancestry. It is an affirmative expression of the Black female experience, calling us to engage in our sacred practices in order to actively remember what this system of white supremacy actively forces us to forget.

When I think of Walker and Dillard, and so many other Black women who attempted to name and articulate an understanding of Black feminism for themselves, I don't just see myself; I see you too! Sure, you would have never called yourself a womanist or even a feminist for that matter. You might have even shrieked at the notion! However, the more I learn about you, and yes, I have been asking questions, I understand that you indeed were at least a nascent womanist. You eschewed gender roles when it wasn't popular to do so. You pushed back on the notion of what it was to be a Black woman at a time when Black women were solely defined by what we could produce through our hands or through our wombs. You were commanding and in charge. You insisted on self-definition and autonomy, and I imagine it drove you crazy that our society's commitment to misogynoir wouldn't allow you to fully realize who you dreamed you could be. You wouldn't allow this country's limiting vision of who you were—a Black woman and a daughter of sharecroppers with limited education—to constrain your vision, so you pushed to create a space for yourself where you could spread your wings and fly, even if just for a little bit. I see a lot of you in me, my fellow Aquarian. I follow in your footsteps, albeit in a less traumatizing way.

Chapter 13

How I wish we had more time. For years, I promised to come home and transcribe your stories. I thought time was on my side. At least, I thought there was time until you got Alzheimer's, which ate away at your body for nearly ten years. Last time I saw you, in 2018, you weren't even talking. But you still looked like the granny I had always known and loved.

I hoped to get to you in 2019, but I didn't make it down to Milwaukee at all that year because I went to Ghana for the summer. I went back for the Year of Return, to be on the soil where our ancestors birthed us. I needed to trace their steps, put my hands in the nooks and crannies of the walls where they were held captive, wade in the water that eventually brought them to this country. And I am so glad that I went. To me, returning to the motherland at least once in our lifetimes, or more if we can swing it, has to be a priority of every single African ascendant. There are pieces of our lives that we cannot make sense of until we behold for ourselves this place that birthed our ancestors.

It was not until I went to Ghana that I started to understand why missions used to be so important to me. Yes, I wanted to preach the Gospel. But more than this, I wanted to leave the United States because there is simply no escaping anti-Blackness and the harm that comes with it here. No, I did not have this analysis when I was seventeen, standing at the bus stop trying to figure out why I wasn't in El Salvador. In the absence of analysis, my body, as a result of growing up on Lisbon Ave in the 1990s and experiencing so much harm, understood what Christina Sharpe (2016) explains as anti-

Blackness being the actual ground that we walk on, the ground from which we try to speak and articulate ourselves. Or in the words of Fanon (1967), anti-Blackness is more than a feeling of inferiority but a feeling of nonexistence. "All those white men in a group, guns in their hands, cannot be wrong. I am guilty. I do not know of what, but I know that I am no good" (p. 139). This is what we have been trying to outrun for generations, and we take up this fantasy of flight in everything that we do because we are drowning in the sea of insurmountable white supremacy and we literally cannot breathe.

The anti-Blackness is real. This is our reality. And yet and still, I wrestle with this reality and cannot accept it as if it is our eternal state. I cannot accept it because then we resign ourselves to perpetual harm that we cannot shake ourselves free from as long as we are on this soil. My longing to be a missionary all of these years, I must conclude, is inextricably tied to wanting to outrun this reality. And Ghana, well, Ghana presented me with the opportunity to imagine the possibility of not just me but all of us boarding that ship one last time, crossing back over the Atlantic, and going back through the Door of No Return to recreate ourselves in the land that birthed us from dirt. I know it won't be perfect, nothing ever is, but I have to imagine, I have to believe, that this life as we currently imagine it isn't all there is.

I am under no illusion that to return means that it is possible to return to an ideal state of what the continent used to be. We have been pushed out of Eden, pushed away from who we might have been before we were made strangers by fellow Africans, so that our bodies could be commodified. We have long resisted the narrative that other Africans were complicit in our oppression; it hurts too much to believe that our own kin betrayed us, but we must face this truth if we hope to heal and be restored to each other. Perhaps, the hope in return then, is not in finding something that is perfect and unstained, but that in spite of finding destruction, greed, and self-interest, we could still be committed to restoration. Because we are worth it! Africa is worth it! And Black people are worth it, wherever we are in the world!

We can't go back to the way things used to be, but we can recover and reclaim the remnants that have been left behind in order to move forward and (re)construct who we want to be. We must do this even when it hurts to look in the historical archive, even when it hurts to (re)member. We can't allow pain to get in the way of us moving forward. Sankofa must become a verb: go back and fetch what is at risk of being left behind, forgotten, discarded, in order to bring it forward to inform our future. I believe that the continent is a place of possibility for us to do this work; our existence in the United States will always demand our blood, as both Critical Race Theory and Afropessimism tell us. And maybe I am even naïve in believing that it could be better somewhere else. But I am willing to be naïve, willing to take a risk, willing to stick my neck out and state that for Africa we must fight, so that all Africans, wherever we are located across the globe, can be free.

It is with the hope of what Africa could be, in the midst of so much strife on the continent, including the End SARS Movement in Nigeria, as well as the horizontal violence that we still experience in the diaspora, that I write these words:

Don't leave Africa
...to the Portuguese, the Dutch, and the British who
pillaged and raped the land
...to the ruling elite who sold us off as strangers
...to the colonizers who renamed and refashioned it
into their own image and who cloistered people
together, creating false identities where there was
distinction between them

Don't leave Africa
...to the politicians who colluded with the enemy to
keep the continent in chains
...to the so-called radicals who dispossessed
Lumumba, Nkrumah, and so many others who could
have really made things better
..to the foreign interest groups—missionaries,
developers, NGOs, and everyone else who claims to
love Africa even as their hands remain clutched to the
diamonds and gold deep within Africa's pockets

Don't leave Africa
...to the military or police
...to the rebels who stole our girls or to the those who
set our churches and mosques ablaze
...to the marauding businessmen dressed in a three-
piece suit only looking to make a buck off of the
suffering of the masses (even when they look like us)
..to the clergy whose promises of eternal salvation
strangely coincide with the size of their wallets

But Leave Africa
...to the dreamers and those who want to make it
better

...to the mothers and fathers who tirelessly work for a greater tomorrow for their children
...to the children who study and to those who can't so that their future can be brighter than their right now

Leave Africa
...to the grandmothers and grandfathers who sacrifice all they have so that their grandchildren can eat
...to the traditionalists whose ceremonies and rituals keep our culture and history alive
...to the inventors, the creatives, the healers, and the teachers whose work help us imagine a world without colonizers
...to the griots who help us keep our stories close to our heart

Leave Africa
...to the Pan-Africanists who never let the dream of a united people die
...to those scattered abroad who keep hoping after all hope is lost that to this place we might one day return
...to those who remain committed to the idea that Africa, our beloved Africa, our mother, our beginning and our end, will be great because we dreamed it into existence. And Africa's great people will know suffering no more.

Leave Africa
...to the people who care more about this vision than power and control or the money in their pockets
...to the passionate, to the lovers, to the ideologues, to the dreamers

...to those willing to go out of their ever loving minds—because they can see that the vision is so close that they can taste it, and it tastes like Heaven

Chapter 14

So no, we did not make it down to Milwaukee for summer. But we planned to come for Thanksgiving. I so desperately wanted to be with family, to not have to cook as much since I was recovering from a surgery I had just had the week before. We were going to stay with one of my sisters, who had been trying to get me to come down for Thanksgiving for years.

It seemed like 2019 would be the year. And I was excited, even as I struggled over the notion of what I would be able to eat since I had recently gone vegan. A snowstorm in Minnesota the day before Thanksgiving kept us home. It ruined all of our plans, in more ways than one. To the store I went, picking up lamb, goat meat, and oxtail—not for my benefit, mind you. I did not like the way things had turned out. I needed to see you. But Minnesota weather was making that impossible.

We weren't able to get there for Christmas either. And I was in my feelings about the whole thing the whole time! This time of year is always difficult for me because I still long for the way things used to be. Sitting around your table every Christmas and being so close to family was one of the most amazing things about my childhood. Sure, I enjoyed the food, we all did. But that was just the icing on top, at least for me it was. I needed the stories, the connection, the ritual of your table that sustained us. And the fact that this is now missing brings me to tears every single year, even as I am raising a family of my own. Because, Granny, this time of year just isn't the same without you.

Then came 2020. You turned eighty-eight on January 26. Big cuz and his family visited you at the nursing home. They bought you flowers and took pictures with you. It was so sweet!

This was four days after my birthday. My dad sent me money to take out the kids for lunch, and then we went to the Winter Carnival in downtown St. Paul. On the way there, we learned that Kobe Bryant and his daughter, Gianna Bryant, were killed in that ghastly plane crash. I am not a basketball fan at all; to be fair I am not a fan of any sports. But I was speechless. I just couldn't help thinking of their last moments as I spent the afternoon ice skating with my children. I still do not have words to describe the energy that defined that day. It felt immensely harrowing that you had to share your day with such tragedy, which seemed to be felt by the whole world.

As it turns out, that same energy ended up defining the whole year. I know I have not even made forty yet, but I can honestly say that 2020 was the weirdest year in the history of the world. Or at least, it was the strangest year I have ever known. By mid-March, many places were in full shut-down mode because of the coronavirus. We started working from home immediately. All of my classes went online, and the kids were also completing their school year online, which disturbed me because I had tried my best to keep them from having their lives dominated by devices.

In mid-April, I called your nursing home to ask about how you were doing in the midst of all of this. I thought about sending you clothes, money, or whatever, but wanted to first find out what you needed. I worried about the impact of

COVID-19 on your body and wanted to ask about your well-being. I never got through.

A week later, as April 24 moved into April 25, I lay awake at night trying to get to sleep. I tossed and turned for what seemed like hours, and finally got up to pray, feeling as if God might have been trying to tell me something. But I wasn't completely sure. It could have just been my nerves. After all, I was holding space for the Kinky Curly Theological Collective later on in the day. Though it wasn't my first time hosting this space, it was my first time hosting it online. So, I prayed, asking God to give me strength to do this thing, and ironically, ended up praying for the well-being of my family as well.

Later on that day, I noticed my cousin repost the picture that was shared on your birthday. In the back of my head, I wondered why, but didn't give myself much space to satisfy my questions.

The next morning, just as church was ending, Auntie let me know that you were gone. I couldn't believe it. I beat my fists into the floor so hard, over and over again, because the reality of your demise was too much to bear. And I wept.

Yes, I know that you had been gone for years. I hadn't had a serious conversation with you since I was pregnant with my son, who is about to turn eight. You just deteriorated that fast. But the thing was, you represented stability. You represented support that I desperately needed. Your prayers and your presence got me through some tough times in this life. I have lived all of my thirty-eight years with you in my life, I don't know what it is to live without you. You weren't just my grandmother; you were a true mother to me, and I will always cherish that.

And I never got to say goodbye. COVID-19 robbed us of that opportunity. Instead, I watched your homegoing service over Zoom. Zoom, Granny. I doubt you even know what that is. It felt insulting to commemorate you like this. But we had no other choice. This pandemic has taken away so many people's agency to say goodbye to their relatives properly.

Although the time has escaped us for now, I know that I will one day have the opportunity to see your face again in heaven. I know that God has prepared for you the most magnificent home. And if I could make a guess, that home is covered in velvety red carpet, with matching pillows to boot. The windows have the same Christmas wreath that you have held onto for years. You have your patio overlooking your expansive backyard. When I come for a visit, you will offer me a soda just as you always do, and I will turn it down, just as I always do since I haven't drunk that diabetes-inducing beverage in over twenty years. But I'll take a slice or two of your wonderful sweet potato pie. Note that I will need it cold with lots of nutmeg.

We'll sit down at your kitchen table eating our pie. I'll pull out my paper and pen so I can write down the stories as you tell them. This time I will be ready. I won't miss it for anything in the world. Until then, come visit me near the lilac tree I planted in the front yard in your honor. It's been there almost a year now and it's growing strong and beautiful, just like you were.

we may have left
but the spirit never left us

the ancestors have continued to guide us
separated by land and sea
they are only a whisper away

some by boat
others by plane
most through death
we all have a way of returning
of going through the door
resting on the land
our ancestors birthed us

enjoy your rest

"For Granny," Excerpted from The Gospel According to a Black Woman © 2020

Incomplete Stories

Conclusion

The passing of my grandmother in 2020, and of her husband in 2016, did not create a wound; instead these deaths re-invigorated wounds that was already there. My grandmother's dining room table, where we gathered Christmas after Christmas, represented the few precious moments when my family felt close. In its absence, it has felt as if we could not be. This has led to intense feelings of loneliness and isolation, feelings that in all honesty were always there. But her passing brought them to the surface and COVID-19 meant that I had to finally face them.

But I am working through them. Little by little. And it's been hard because all of the coping mechanisms that have brought me to this point are no longer working. Resiliency got me here, but healing is going to have to carry me the rest of the way in order to ensure that I actually break the generational patterns that continue to lead to the same outcomes. For me, (re)membering is an act of healing!

This is perhaps the number one reason why the (re)constructing of my family's story is so important. I have needed to look at my experiences through that history so that I can better understand how I got here. My quest is to figure out the root of the loneliness and despair that always seems to settle in the middle of my chest, an experience that either leaves me speechless or sitting in a pool of tears. As Resmaa Menakem, author of *My Grandmother's Hands*, always says: I am not defective. Something happened to me and my ancestors. In spite of what has happened, I am loving and lovable. And I deserve meaningful and reciprocal relationships. And we all do. I know that I am not the only one who faces these struggles, who longs for the extended tables full of loved ones, or the backyards full of relatives to commemorate all of our celebrations. My challenge to us all, as I first challenge myself, is to lean into the discomfort, the pain, to admit how lonely we feel, and that we do not even know where to start to rebuild the trust between us as a people that was destroyed by the slave trade. We must admit the extent to which slavery impeded our ability to relate to one another. Speaking to the rupture in our relationships, Orlando Patterson states that, "every slave knew that, to survive emotionally and physically, she sometimes had to make choices that betrayed her relations with others. This slowly and corrosively undermined all interactions" (p. x).

If, and only if, we were honest with ourselves, we would accept how Patterson's words continue to ring true. This is because, while slavery created the rupture, the continual degradation of Black life reifies it. Even with the best of intentions, we struggle to find our way back to each other, not only within our own family systems but also within our community as a whole. I believe that (re)constructing our familial and cultural narratives is one of many acts that puts us in the process of healing so that we can find our way back. We do this through (re)membering, as both Dillard and Dunbar-Ortiz urge us. And in (re)membering, we must understand that what we will uncover is not always pleasant and may evoke feelings of rage and despair. This is why we have suppressed the memories so long.

A word on the (re)membering process: As I finished the narratives found in these pages, I recalled that I had actually interviewed my grandmother about her life on two separate occasions—once during undergrad in 2003 and once in seminary in 2007. Because I tend to hold onto everything I write, I knew that I probably had these interviews documented somewhere. So, I went looking and found the 2003 paper in a file that has many of my papers from undergrad and seminary, though I still have not located the paper from 2007. Not finding the 2007 paper where I thought it would be, I went searching for it in a trunk that my mother bought for me when I left Milwaukee in 2001 for school. In the trunk, I found my paternal grandmother's obituary, as well as the obituary of my maternal grandfather—pieces of my family history that I did not know I had.

But I also found the journals from my youth, starting at about ninth grade, as well as pictures that help me know a little bit more about who I am and who I have always been.
I look at the pictures, the stories and journals, the archive of my family, and know I was called to weave together our stories and create new ones. Storyteller, writer, poet, preacher, theologian—all of my life's work from the time I was younger has led me to this point. When I was in ninth grade, singing in the choir at church, I used to ask the choir director why I felt compelled to write so much. I don't think he had much of an answer, but I do know that he affirmed that maybe I would do something with all of these words someday. Now I understand. I understand my calling, I understand who I am, and it is all because I went looking for the woman who has held such significance in my life. In looking for her, my grandmother, I found me.

I am so honored that you decided to join me in my process of (re)membering and (re)construction. It has not been an easy one for me, and I know that as I recounted my story, you were confronted with your own. Don't shy away from the discomfort; instead, let's commit to go through this process of understanding together, so we don't have to face these histories on our own.

Be blessed.

Part Two
A Black Woman's Journey of (Re)membrance

In 2018, Ghanian President Nana Akufo-Addo announced before the United Nations that 2019 would be the Year of Return for Africans across the diaspora. This was important because 2019 marked the four hundredth year since Africans were stolen and forcibly enslaved in the British colonies that would become the United States. Although Africans had been enslaved by the Portuguese and Spanish throughout the Americas, Caribbean, and Europe prior to the oft-quoted 1619, this commemoration gave Africans across the diaspora whose ancestors experienced this horror—or Maafa—an opportunity to actively engage in the process of (re)membering and reclamation of self, recognizing that there is not unilateral agreement among us about the actual start of our enslavement in the Americas and also recognizing that even prior to enslavement, Africans had been in the Americas.

I can't quite remember what I was doing when I heard the announcement back in October of 2018. Most likely, I was just getting home from class—as I had started my PhD program that fall. As my husband filled me in on President Akufo-Addo's words, I remember thinking to myself that I had to find a way to get to Ghana in the next several months. Meditating on the prospect of going, I penned these words:

> Rushing out the door, two kids in tow
> Carrying backpacks, lunch bags, water bottles and
> one cup of tea for me
> Piling into the car
> Buckling the youngest one who always seems to need
> a boost of help to get him going
> Speeding down Larpenteur

Praying the cops don't see me because there still is
that one ticket I didn't pay
But I will ... soon

Radio is blasting, can't remember the song
Somewhere between Lexington and 280, my mind
starts to wander to its happy place and all of the
anxieties of the last hour dissipate because I'm
thinking of you ... dreaming of you ... rehearsing the
same dream in my mind that I have been conjuring
up for the last four years

I started dreaming when Mike Brown was shot, and
then more when his killer got off. My dream took on
new dimensions after Charleston, intensified the
more every single time one of us fell to the ground

The dream grew in the days, weeks, and months
leading up to the election. Expanded as the
deplorables tore apart policies my ancestor's blood
paid for. Reinvigorated with every single faux
commitment to racial justice expressed by those well
meaning liberals, and even some of us who weren't so
much as interested in dismantling the master's house
as we were living in it.

No matter the cycle, the season, the news feature, the
misfortune, the dream has held steady. It has felt
unattainable, irrational, and close all at the same
time. And now, after 400 years, it's within reach.
They said we wouldn't make it. That we wouldn't get
here. But the dream is no longer a thought, it's on the
horizon, just beyond the sun, just beyond where I-94

meets the streets, pushing me out of the dream and thrusting me back into reality.

Ms. Walker, bump Canada. I'm taking mama 'em to Africa.
"Dreaming of Home," Excerpted from The Gospel According to a Black Woman *(Adedayo, 2020)*

In many ways, these words became a prayer over the next few months. I applied for a travel-abroad opportunity to Ghana through my school and was accepted, but I just couldn't get my money right in time. But another opportunity presented itself and although money was still an issue, this time felt more sure. I could feel it in my soul even though I wasn't sure about how. So I went for it.

Before I knew it, I was making the first, second, and last deposits to go on this ten-day trip with a team of people led by Planting People, Growing Justice. I renewed my passport, which had expired ten years prior, and got all of the immunizations one body could handle. And I shopped and packed and made sure I had all of the snacks (believe me, I had all the snacks)—doing everything possible to make sure that I was prepared for this journey.

But the biggest preparation was that of my heart and spirit. The last time I was on the continent was back in 2007, and it was a trip that absolutely changed the prospect of my life. Going to Rwanda and the Democratic Republic of Congo, places where I so easily fit in, was easily a second conversion experience that woke me up from the slumber of Evangelism and its blatant tendency to ignore God's heart for justice.

I am still reaping the rewards of that investment of time and resources that I spent in 2007 on reconnecting to the land my ancestors were stolen from. Even though I did not have the same political astuteness that I have today. I knew that the journey in 2019 would be even more impactful. I took that journey even more seriously, spending a lot of time in prayer and meditation so that my heart would be open to all that the ancestors had for me.

In going, I committed myself to transcribing my experiences so that I could balance my experiences with my research studies through the autoethnography. The autoethnography would also help me answer a growing inquiry around how returning to the continent for cultural self-study enhances the academic work of African-ascended women. It would also help me understand how the experiences of the past—both prior to and after the Maafa—were informing how we as African-ascended people were showing up in the present. I first encountered autoethnography, also called self-study, as a result of a fellowship that I had with the Cultural Wellness Center in 2018.

That fellowship afforded me the opportunity to spend a year reflecting on myself—including my people, my family, and my history. Although I have long engaged in the process of critical self-reflection and analysis, this fellowship took my practice to a new level. And so, when I started my PhD program in the fall of 2018, I found myself gravitating towards autoethnography almost instantly because of my commitment to using my narrative as a tool for change in and outside of higher education. I agreed with H. Richard Milner IV (2007) when he said that, "telling our stories is indeed a matter of survival: only by telling and listening, storying and restorying can we begin the process of constructing a common world" (p. 605).

Prior to starting the PhD program, I launched a community-based effort for African-ascended women that was centered on the premise that Milner proposed. Called the Aya Collective, formerly the Kinky Curly Theological Collective, it endeavored to give space for African-ascended women to tell our stories as a means to counter the narratives that were dominant in the Church, higher education, and other institutions about who we were. What was and remains to be fascinating about this space is that the stories among so many diverse, unique, African-ascended women were so similar. Hearing each other talk back to ourselves about what we collectively experienced felt affirming, in the same way that reading Anzaldua's *Borderlands/La Frontera: The New Mestiza* (1987) and hooks' (1994/2017) *Teaching to Transgress* was affirming.

Stories of individuals that speak to the collective experience are liberating because it reassures us that we are not some oddity nor are we overreacting when we speak to what we've been through. Experiences such as these have deepened my resolve to leverage individual stories to speak about the collective experience. Additionally, my individual testimony would be a way to build not only my own faith but the faith of other African-ascended people.

Although Anzaldua was Chicana, I found resonance in her compelling story of navigating the space between her indigenous past and the Mexican people's suffering as a result of colonialization. Jimenez (2020) says, "there is a need for telling stories from the past, to reclaim the past, to give testimony to the injustices of the past, and to reinscribe local knowledge" (p. 784). These stories end up being counter stories, one of the tenets of Critical Race Theory, that resist dominant (and mostly repressive) narratives about who we as a people are.

Committed to the autoethnographic process in my study and in my work, I got on that plane to Ghana on June 27, two days after my son's birthday and suffering from a summer cold (who gets those). I was slightly anxious because I had never been away from my children for so long, and I was also excited for what would unfold over the next few weeks. Deep in the clouds hovering somewhere over North Africa, I wrote:

> We are in the air and are about to pass over the continent by way of North Africa—Tunisia, Algeria, and Morocco. I am delighted to be here as, until I got to the plane yesterday, it all felt surreal. This is the moment I have been waiting for since I first heard about it in October.
>
> You ordained this moment for me. God, from the beginning of time, you knew my ancestors would cross the Atlantic 400 years ago. And you knew that I would look white supremacy and racism squarely in the face and declare these forces of evil powerless. You knew I would be doing this work with the City of Minneapolis. The time has come for our healing and deliverance, and I believe we have to reconnect with this place of our origins in order to find that rest.
>
> If we are connected to the land, if the land is a living, breathing life-producing thing, we have to reconnect

back to it. The Spirit of our ancestors long for that rest. We have to get them back to the land.

After 400 years, I am here to bring my ancestors who longed for this day. I remember those who left, not knowing where they were going but knowing that they were leaving the only place they knew. I am going for them and so that I can move forward with remembering/bringing to consciousness who we were before slavery, so we have a much more adequate understanding of who we are, what we are building into the future.

We need a different vision. Continue to shape in me what that vision is.

Excerpts from the journal

The following stories depict my experiences in Ghana in the summer of 2019. I chose these entries because they were the most meaningful to me and also represent a diversity of experiences over the twelve-day period. The first entry is about my experience seeing one of the remaining dungeons where Africans were held in Accra.

Day 3: June 30, 2019

As we were out sightseeing after church today, a man stopped us and asked if we would like a tour. He would charge us twenty cedis each. We said yes. He was very knowledgeable and told us about the history of that particular area, which used to be one of the many (over forty) slave ports in Ghana alone. The one he showed us was previously owned by the British and was named Jamestown after King James in England. I think he said it was established in 1611 or 1617, but I recognize the connection. This James also commissioned a Bible in 1611 and Jamestown, VA, would also be named after him. We need to do more investigation of this James and how tied he was to the slave trade as I had never made the connection before today. Because then you have to investigate how he translated the Bible and the decisions that were made and how this version was used to oppress Africans who were enslaved.

Our guide talked about the slave dungeon that was in that site in particular, and how there was an underground route that led out to the water where those who were enslaved took their last bath before getting on the boat. I took a picture of this and am quite disappointed that it did not save. It felt surreal to walk this same land that our ancestors walked. I wonder what they felt in their hearts before they left and if they could comprehend what was happening. I reflected:

> Was this the land where my ancestors walked?
> Was this the water their hands touched?
> Was this the sky their eyes met as they petitioned
> God for their release? Was this the door they went
> through to never return again?
> Am I their only hope of coming back and making
> amends?
> Of walking through that door
> Praying to that God
> Bathing in that water
> Letting my bare feet touch the dusty ground
> Am I their only hope of healing this historical
> memory so that those coming after me breathe a little
> bit easier, move through the world a little more

gracefully, sleep a little bit more soundly?

Could our soul begin to rest because we came?
Could we find peace because we were here?

And I wonder who my ancestors prayed to. I wonder what was in their thoughts. So many people didn't make it out alive and yet, I am here. Four hundred years later. I am a living example of all those who survived. I don't know how but know that God did and that God answered the prayers of survival and endurance, though we cannot make sense of why God didn't answer the prayers of deliverance. Coming back feels like an opportunity for coming together, like Nehemiah looking at the structure of things so we can build and move forward.

Day 4: July 1, 2019—Reflections on the Water
The Spirit keeps the memories of the ancestors alive. There is so much that I want to say about today. I will start with gratitude and go from there. I remain thankful for being in this space in this year. It is not only symbolic but a spiritual necessity to bring us healing and redemption.

I want to start by talking about the water. Oh my God, the water. Arriving into Elmina at the Coconut Grove and seeing that we are staying on the ocean is something in and of itself. I want as much time with this water as I can possibly get. I felt the Spirit as soon as I stepped onto the sand with my bare feet. I can't swim and was fully clothed so I did not go all the way in. But as I started singing "Our God is an awesome God," the waves came and caught me. The bottom of my pants got soaked. What a powerful energy! I felt as if my ancestors were speaking, were welcoming me home, inviting me in, which was absolutely amazing and refreshing. I wanted to cry tears of joy, sorrow, and disbelief all at the same time. I knew we were supposed to go to the river where our enslaved ancestors took their last bath today. But we actually needed to be here, as this water is our watershed. This water carries the memory of who we were prior to enslavement. This land gave us life. I need to walk the road my ancestors walked and first, I need to have the historical imagination to understand who they were before they were stolen or traded.

The waves are still speaking. They are still making melodies. Give me the heart, the mind, and the spirit to hear. I need to hear you God. I need to hear from the ancestors. I need to take it all in.

I also wanted to cry during Dr. Ebenezer's lecture, understanding the role that Africa has played in this horror. We keep trying to reconcile ourselves to that fact and make sense of the nonsensical, but it does not work. If we tell and write the story, we can help ourselves come to grips with the fact that Africans were complicit in the oppression enacted by the Europeans even if they could not comprehend the gravity of it. That's going to take a lot of work but the opportunity once we do, to bring ourselves back into relationship with each other, to heal the wounds, the heartache that we feel because of how we have treated each other, is tremendous. We have to find our way back to each other, we have to find our way back home and we have to find our way back to you.

Day 5: July 2, 2019—The Door of Return

I couldn't sleep very well last night. That is not completely unusual as I have not been able to sleep well most nights besides when we first arrived. But still, I wonder about the impact on my heart, what my spirit was preparing for, knowing what I would face today.

I want to take things slowly so that I can take everything in, everything that the Spirit above and my ancestors have for me. I want to move slowly so that I don't miss anything on account of rushing, not paying attention, being aloof. I want to hear what the Spirit of God is speaking and I want to hear my ancestors' voices. For the first time I am paying attention and I want to hear.

I know that they have been leading and guiding me back to this place. Everything I have done has been preparation for this. The first time I traveled abroad to El Salvador I hated it. The shock of the place was disorienting. I wanted to go home. I remember praying at Castillo Del Rey for your help and guidance because I couldn't make it. But I did and I loved it, so that when I went back to the US back home, I wondered what God was doing for me in America. That was precisely twenty years ago. I went to college in 2001, with my mind fixed on being a missionary. From El Salvador, I went to Argentina, England, Guatemala, Rwanda, Democratic Republic of the Congo, and Kenya, all in seven years. When a friend of mine first asked me if I wanted to go to Africa I said yes. That trip to the continent in 2007 changed my life. I promised to come back and it took me twelve years to get here. I now understand why.

From the first time I left the States for El Salvador, I knew my life existed beyond the confines of our border. At the time, my imagination only took me as far as missions work—I was genuinely interested in the gospel but I also wanted to go. To be here, not knowing that deep in my heart, this is what I actually longed for is overwhelming.

My husband has been saying it forever, but now I am convinced, we have to move here. My soul is at peace here. My feet stand on holy land and I know this is for me. This is for my family. This is for us as a people. To come back as the children of Israel went back after living in Babylon. To come back as did Garvey, DuBois, and so many others who have taken up Ghana as permanent residence. Our watershed is calling us home.

I have always been African. Africa was born in me. My father named me Ebony—shiny, Black wood—which set off my destiny. He didn't know, but God did. The ancestors did. The ancestors knew this is the path I would walk, so here I am. Here I am God.

I am so mesmerized by this water, God. It is incredibly captivating. Our ancestors are speaking through the water, God. Our ancestors are speaking. I still haven't written about the actual activities of today—I will. They were heavy going through them but I have to come back and document. For God's sake.

Day 7: July 4, 2019

I have not journaled in a few days and feel compelled to write out my thoughts. We saw the second castle at Elmina yesterday. It was much bigger than the castle at Cape Coast. It was initially built for trading before it was converted to slavery activities in the 1500s. The castle at Elmina was built in 1485 by the Portuguese. It is the oldest one in Ghana. The castle at Cape Coast was built in 1665 by the English. It took fifty years to complete. The Castle at Cape Coast is surrounded by canons to protect it from the Europeans. There were many things that were similar between the two places—including the dungeons, the rape of women, the place they would send slaves to die who resisted. There is a dungeon for men and two for women—one dungeon was where they would menstruate. The one for men held 1000, the one for women, 300.

One of the male dungeons that we saw was at one time piled high with feces. Even though the site has now been cleaned up the waste is still very much a part of the floor. There were four segments of this dungeon. The last segment was closest to the tunnels where men who were fit would be selected to go through the journey of slavery across the Atlantic. Women were brutalized and raped and those who resisted were punished through solitary confinement. If a woman got pregnant, she wouldn't be taken on the journey but would go offsite to give birth, was sometimes freed, other times taken care of for ten years before being put into captivity again. The biracial children were freed.

The level of inhumanity and breaking of the spirit is striking to me—our guide said that over twenty million Africans were transported to the Americas and the Caribbean. But since one in three made it to that point, at least forty million died between being stolen from their lands to the Atlantic—many in the slave castles. Was it really cost effective to treat the Africans so inhumanely? Or was it pure evil and greed? I think it was evil and a breaking of the spirit to let Africans know how much they were so regarded by the Europeans. I get that slavery is an old institution and was practiced here but why treat someone, anyone, so poorly, so awfully as the Europeans did the Africans.

What was the hate and jealousy buried so deep in the Europeans' hearts that they treated others this way? This was not and is not normal and we can't claim that it was. There was something unique and specific about the slave trade that made it so awful, that is not easily explained away. And because whiteness is constructed against anti-Blackness, the brutality continues. The brutality is not only driven by profit but a lust for power, control over another human life.

Day 8: July 5, 2020 - Residue of Enslavement
This idea of slave identity is expressed in an essay written by the late Katie Cannon in her essay—"The Old Ship of Zion"—in *My Soul is a Witness.* "The dominant legal and social attitude was that slaves were to be kept ignorant, living on marginal existence, fed or famished, clothed or left naked, shelter or unsheltered as served the slaveholder ..." (p. 20).

Her statement here, which continues to describe the slave identity, is telling. It was not enough to enslave Africans and force them to labor and bear children against their will. There was a whole piece around indoctrination and subjugation that went into it as well. The idea of Africans as innately inferior to Europeans, later codified into a racial caste system, took slavery to a whole new level.

We must not only address slavery as an institution—we also have to address the brutality and sheer inhumanity extracted upon others for profit and pleasure. Why did they have to lock us in dungeons with barely enough water, air, and food for months on end. Why let us live in waste? Or deprive us of air until we die? It wasn't because of money; it was because they could. When we reduce racism to capitalism/profit alone, we miss the fact that some of the brutality had nothing to do with money, but everything to do with controlling the mind, the body, the will of Africans—which continues until this day. Current police brutality is a matter of the will and pleasure, the attitudes exhibited by officers like the ones who killed Sandra Bland are the same attitudes that existed in these slave castles—don't challenge authority, don't push back, if you do it will be dangerous and can most certainly lead to death.

The white man has been trying to get us to submit to him from day one. Submit to the physical, sexual, and mental violence at the risk of increased violence.

Day 10: July 6, 2019—Traumatic Memories
As harmful/painful as the experience of trauma is, one of the most destructive things is to lose memory of that trauma altogether. To be unable to articulate what happened, the horror and abuse, to be unable to testify how you got over it and survived so that generations coming after you will know, is crippling.

When I think about my grandmother's Alzheimer's, I feel like this. It is a loss of memory and family history that we won't ever be able to recover. This makes me sad and it makes me sadder that our family is so isolated, so fragmented and broken, that I am not sure we would be able to get those stories from somewhere else.

When I think about the slave trade and our family's experience since being in the Americas, I think about this. We all experienced the interruption of the slave trade, but what produced the isolation and loss of memory? Where did the trauma get locked in our bodies instead of passing through? No, we did not take our trauma out on each other by violence/abuse/incest—at least to my knowledge—but we did shut ourselves out from each other. What happened that was so awful that we turned away from each other instead of to each other, so we could find healing? I want to heal those memories.

My desire is to heal the memories for myself and my children. My desire is to create the community that does not live in fear of one another but can trust one another. I believe that all of the experiences in my life are leading up to this point. I want to see and hear from you God. I can't do this without you.

Making Sense of Memory

In analyzing the autoethnographic narratives, I primarily draw on two theoretical lenses: Endarkened Feminism Epistemology (EFE) and African Centered Pedagogy. EFE, as conceptualized and defined by Dillard (2012), "articulates how reality is known when based in the historical roots of global Black feminist thought" (p. 59). In Dillard's 2016 article "Turning the Ships Around: A Case Study of (Re)Membering as Transnational Endarkened Feminist Inquiry and Praxis for Black Teachers," she puts forth the notion of (re)membering as the process of (re)searching, (re)visioning, (re)cognizing, (re)presenting, and (re)claiming, which is helpful in recounting my own experiences in Ghana.

The process of (re)searching is probably the most important component for me in relation to Ghana. Here Dillard suggests that (re)searching "involves seeking, looking, and searching for something about Black heritage and/or culture that is believed will teach us something new" (p. 411). This process defined my entire trip, as I constantly searched for experiences that would teach me something new. I believe this is one reason that my notes overall leaned more on the informational side of things than on how I felt in my body. In addition, the days were so jam-packed with activity that I found myself too emotionally exhausted at the end of the day to recount more than the facts of the experiences.

(Re)visioning was another component that really came into play in my experiences. Dillard states that (re)visioning "involves an expansion of our current worldview of Black people, culture, and knowledge" (p. 411). This showed up for me primarily in regard to Dr. Ebenezer's lecture, understanding the role that some African chiefs played in enslavement. His lecture was a hard pill to swallow because then it meant that Africans who had practiced slavery prior to European influence were also complicit in the harm that was visited on Black bodies (though not in the same way white people were complicit—after all there is a particular brutality that defines the transatlantic slave trade that is not seen anywhere else). The idea that Africans participated in our enslavement is a source of so much cognitive dissonance for Black people that we do not often talk about it without getting immensely angry and shutting down. I myself can testify to how my body feels such tension when the topic is broached. But this is the (re)visioning I believe that Dillard is talking about here, having a comprehensive view of who we are as well as our history, while not letting the Europeans off the hook.

My story is also indicative of the (re)cognizing process, which involves expanding our thinking about who Black people are and what we have accomplished, and the (re)presenting process, putting our understanding of Black identities in the world in fuller ways. However, in addition to (re)searching, (re)claimation is one of the most resounding components of my story, namely the process of going back and forth to claim our legacy as African ascended people. The following line in the story speaks to this the loudest:

> I have always been African. Africa was born in me. My father named me Ebony—shiny, Black wood—which set off my destiny. He didn't know, but God did. The ancestors did. The ancestors knew this is the path I would walk so here I am. Here I am, God.

This sort of reclamation would not have come without the cultural self-study and the experience in Ghana. In a sense, I have felt that I was separated from my identity as an African at times. Being able to unequivocally state my Africanness that was birthed in me, rather than me seeking it, was a significant shift in the understanding of my identity.

But of course, this sense of identity is paramount to an African-centered pedagogy (ACP). ACP is defined by Bethea as a cultural framework that is "shaped by specific cosmological (understanding of the universe), ontological (nature of being), epistemological (knowledge) orientations, axiological (values) commitments … that exist across time" (2018, p. 306). Atta (2018) defines an African-centered perspective as one grounded in an African worldview that "recognizes the presence of a Higher Power or Creator … a holistic mind-body-spirit connection, understanding that everything in the Universe is interconnected in Oneness" (p. 228).

For Bethea, ACP is about claiming what is known more than about gaining new knowledge. That claiming has to be rooted in (re)membering, as there is so much that we have forgotten as a result of the distance of time compounded by trauma, and the force to assimilate in ways that protect hegemonic, mainstream pedagogies. "Thus, (re)membering becomes a radical response to our individual and collective fragmentation" (Dillard 2012, p. 17).

Two questions around (re)membering that emerged from my writings were in regard to (re)membering who we were prior to the Maafa and (re)membering to make sense of the brutality of enslavement and its aftermath. Having already addressed the question of what happened before the Maafa, I now turn to the questions of (re)membering that center the pain of what happened over generations. My commitment here stems from the prevalence of trauma in my family of origin as I try to piece together fragmented pieces of a story in hopes of finding some semblance of wholeness. In my reflection, I recounted how disconnected we were from these narratives as a result of my grandmother having Alzheimer's for nearly a decade. Now that we have lost her for good to eternity, the loss feels even more significant and the need to address these questions feels ever more urgent.

At the same time, however, there is this African way of knowing that attests to the spirit keeping the memory of the ancestors alive (Terborg-Penn, 2001). I believe that this is one of the reasons that I was particularly drawn to the water while in Ghana, both the river where our ancestors took their last bath as well as the Atlantic Ocean. Bodies of water hold memory. But so does the land. This is why I wanted to walk barefoot on a land that I had never been on, out of a desire to hear and connect. And it is also why in my grandmother's passing, I have been more vigilant about getting into my own garden and creating my own sustaining rituals to call forth memory. Here I have been most inspired by Jackson's (2001) essay recounting her family's connection to the soil, a ritual that has become her own: "For with the passage of each season, my backyard paradise has become a spiritual sanctuary. It is where I am most in touch with myself and with God" (p. 48).

It is not only the water and the land that remember; our bodies remember too. Our bodies remember our beginnings, our history, our culture. Though we are disconnected from these beginnings and history because of our separation from the land and the language, we still carry the semblance of them in our bones. People such as the Gullah Geechee along the coasts North Carolina, South Carolina, Georgia, and Florida are one visible example of this as their practice of cultivating rice, and even some of their songs, can be directly traced to Sierra Leone and Senegal. It has taken researchers committed to articulating what we have retained from our ancient past, (re)membering, to make these connections and bring it into our consciousness.

Concluding Thoughts

In many ways, this study is the beginning of my attempts to use autoethnography as a research method to examine my experiences as an ascendant of Africans who were enslaved. EFE and ACP are two theoretical lenses that I use to analyze these experiences, understanding that my individual, unique experiences are also a reflection of the collective. This includes the experiences inside of my family system, as all ascendants of Africans who were enslaved have had to be resilient in the face of slavery, Jim Crow, and everything else that followed. And all of us have lost access to our cultural ways of knowing and organizing the world as a result. Finding similarities, unity even, amidst the diversity of our experiences and backgrounds as African-ascendant people is the best way to examine the structural injustices that have brought us to this current moment and move forward.

(Re)membering who we are culturally, as explained in Dillard's EFE framework, is not only a tool for analyzing our experiences as African-ascended people, it is also a tool for reconfiguring the field of education, including higher education. Atta (2018) emphasizes the role that the African-centered worldview plays in putting an end to the miseducation of the dominated because it centers the experiences of African peoples. Bethea (2018) likewise speaks to how the re-Africanization process enriches the academic process for African-ascended peoples, supported through self-study, rigorous study of the work of Black scholars, and setting our feet on African soil. Application of these fields of thought suggest that African-ascended scholars will emerge from the academy, and other institutions that we labor in, with solutions rooted in a deeper, more comprehensive analysis of where we are going.

When I think about my educational experiences up until my PhD work, I can attest to the fact that I have never been able to examine so deeply, so intently, my cultural legacy. That left me ill-equipped to do adequate work in my own community. Fortunately, in the time between the completion of my master's and the start of my PhD, an eight-year gap, I started the process of making up for my own miseducation through rigorous study. This PhD program is a continuation of what I started privately. I am now doing the work that my soul must have, not only for my soul, but for the souls of my ancestors, my community, and those coming after me. Because of my commitment to (re)membering and looking back and forth to claim and assert our legacy as African-ascendant people, we will all be better for it.

Part Three
Go Back and Get It

Incomplete Stories

Every fourth Friday, for at least the last four years, my husband and I have participated in a community-based educational forum hosted by Solidarity Twin Cities, called Nu Skool for African American Thought. My husband started going first and attended regularly for years. Because our children were quite small at the time, I only dropped in every now and again, especially because when the group first started meeting, it was in the backroom of the old Golden Thyme, a coffee shop on Selby in St. Paul, MN. If anyone has ever been there, you know that the room is small and is not really conducive to very active children who need space to move around in.

But about four years ago, maybe a little less than that, the group started meeting at the High School for Recording Arts. The space in this building is much bigger and accommodating to everyone, not just small children, making it possible for me to be in the space on a regular basis. As a family, we made a ritual out of being there, only missing if we were out of town or one of us was sick. We made this a priority because we were building community with other folks and because we were receiving quality education about the experience and history of us as Black people that we were hard pressed to find in other places.

Every time that we attend feels like a Sankofa experience, or an experience of helping us to remember who we are and what has happened to us. The horrors of enslavement, Jim Crow, and ongoing police brutality. The struggles for freedom and liberation. The joy found in reclaiming our culture and spirituality, creating and making a name for ourselves, and celebrating how we have gotten *ovah* generation after generation after generation.

These acts of (re)membering, as presented through each speaker, are the essence of what Sankofa is. Originating from the Akan people in Ghana, Sankofa means to "go back and get what is at risk of being left behind." The symbol itself is in the shape of a bird, with a head that is turned backwards but with its feet facing forward, meaning that in order to move forward, in order to know where you are going, you have to remember where you've been. You have to remember who you are.

I see this call to remember, to Sankofa, all throughout the biblical text, including Mark 14.1–9. In verse nine of this text, Jesus's words to the disciples who jeered at this woman with the alabaster box, who was lavishly pouring out its contents on Jesus, were that because of her deeds, she would be remembered in the context of spreading the gospel over the entire world. I love the way that the New Revised Standard Version (NRSV) Bible translation puts it, suggesting that this woman's act is key to the gospel itself and that is what we are to remember.

But if we are honest with ourselves, we have not done a good job remembering or uplifting this woman. Most sermons that I have ever heard about her focus on Luke's translation of this episode, drawing attention to this woman's sinfulness and occupation as a sex worker. In Luke's gospel, found in chapter seven, verses 36–50, the emphasis is on the forgiveness that Jesus extends to her for her actions. But in Mark, as well as in Matthew and John, the focus is not on what Jesus gives but rather on what Jesus receives.

This is what I want us to focus on so that we can understand just what Jesus is calling us to remember, to go back and get. Let's start at the top of Mark 14 and work our way down. First of all, the writer tells us that it's a few days before the Passover and the chief priests and religious scribes are plotting to kill Jesus. We do not know if Jesus was told about this latest development, but we can assume that he knows because he has predicted his death several times before in Mark chapters eight, nine, and ten.

Now verse three tells us that while Jesus is at Bethany, in the house of Simon the leper, this woman comes in with this alabaster jar of really expensive oil. Mark does not tell us the woman's name. In fact, the only gospel writer that names her is Luke, who assumes her to be Mary, the sister of Martha and Lazarus. Because the chapter of Mark was written first, and he traveled with Jesus—though he wasn't a disciple—-I am partial to his translation and so I don't assume she is Mary. But I feel inclined to give this woman a name, an identity, to push back on society's tendency to erase the experiences and contributions of marginalized women. So I call her Roxanne.

Roxanne has this expensive jar of oil, breaks the jar, and pours the anointment on Jesus's head. Let us take notice of what she is engaging in and the office that she is functioning in at this moment; she is functioning as a priest, contrasted with the priests and religious leaders found in verses one and two of Mark 14, who are wanting to do Jesus in.

You see, even though anointing oil was often used as a token of hospitality throughout the ancient world, including in ancient Egypt or Kemet, Greece, and Rome, in the Hebrew tradition, it was used exclusively for priests, with a strict forbiddance of it being used on an outsider or common people. In addition, oil was used by priests to anoint prophets, priests, and kings into their offices. Meaning that, especially in this time, it was a male-dominated ritual. So here we have this Roxanne, potentially a sex worker, with no formal religious authority, doing something outside of religious custom, anointing Jesus. In her act, even if she does not recognize it, she is claiming spiritual authority while simultaneously extending that authority to Jesus, affirming that he is prophet, priest, and king!

The disciples miss it because the disciples miss everything. They have missed all of the clues that Jesus has given about his death, and still to some extent think that he is going to topple the oppressive Roman government by setting up a kingdom on earth. So it's not necessarily strange that they are pushing back against this woman here! What is different, or peculiar, is that most likely it is Judas himself who is pushing back, stating that the money could have been spent on behalf of the poor, which is not only ironic because Judas was a thief, but also because Roxanne may have been poor herself. As a single woman in a society such as this, if she wasn't poor, she was probably near poor—one catastrophe away from total ruin. And if Roxanne is a sex worker, as Luke seems to suggest, poverty is definitely an issue for her; in a highly sexist society, the opportunities for women outside of the home of their fathers or husbands simply were not abundant. And so for this Judas to suggest that this woman's priorities are off tells us that he isn't really clued in to the poor that he claims to care so much about.

Rightly so, Jesus pushes back, saying that the disciples, or Judas, should leave Roxanne alone because she has "performed a good service for me." Again, I prefer the NRSV translation here because the NRSV emphasizes that Jesus is receiving something from this woman; it's not just about her kindness. In fact, Roxanne is going out of her way to prepare Jesus for his burial. She is doing what the priests refused to do; they did not want to have anything to do with Jesus, and she is doing what the disciples could not do because again, they miss everything. Whether or not she recognizes the weight of what she is doing is not important. What is important is that Roxanne feels something in her spirit compelling her to act, compelling her to risk her reputation, risk her comfort, risk being ridiculed and even cast aside, in service of a higher purpose.

For her service, Jesus declares that she is to be remembered in the context of the gospel. And you have to wonder if this is one of the things that finally pushes Judas over the edge, realizing that if Jesus is to go any further, he is going to render irrelevant, and possibly even destroy, the patriarchal power structure that was not only evident in Judaism but across the ancient world. Look at Jesus's track record up until this moment—yes, he has healed men, women, and children alike. But he has been particularly partial towards women, drawing them near when others have disregarded, abused, and exploited them. And he keeps doing it, forsaking societal and religious customs to communicate divine love and acceptance regardless of how sinful everyone else has made them out to be.

What would that mean for men like Judas, if all of a sudden women had all of this autonomy and agency over their own bodies, over their dreams and visions? If women, not just those who had it together but who were messy like Roxanne, were accepted by society, how would that shake things up? Consider the Samaritan woman in John 4 who had five husbands, the Syrophoenician woman who Jesus initially denied, or the woman caught in an act of adultery in John 8. Jesus refused to treat all of these women in ways that society said that they should be treated, completely reframing their reality, not only for their liberation but for us all. Think about it: the Syrophoenician woman's act of bravery in challenging Jesus on his cultural bias opened up the gospel to those outside of Judaism long before the Apostle Paul came along. The Samaritan woman's vulnerability with Jesus opened up the gospel to her entire community, which had been routinely ostracized. And Roxanne's act found in Mark 14 today is the representation, the embodiment, of the gospel itself; that yes, Jesus died to save the world, and that if it wasn't for these women willing to be used by God in some radical ways, putting their bodies on the line, that the world would never know.

I really wanted to talk about (re)membering in the context of this writing. And my offering to us is this: we have to remember these narratives, we have to remember these women that Jesus routinely brought near even when history renders their stories irrelevant and unimportant. We have to Sankofa and go back and get them! But not only these women, but the stories and narratives that we set down somewhere because they did not seem convenient to carry around. We allow ourselves to forget so much; we've been seduced to forget. Sometimes we forget because the memories hurt, memories of our exclusion and oppression, memories of waiting on the world to validate something God affirmed in us twenty years ago. But sometimes we forget because we think it's easier to navigate a very patriarchal, white supremacist society if we leave our cultural and spiritual identities at the door and don't draw attention to the fire inside of ourselves, lest we invite critique and punishment as Roxanne did in Mark 14. It's not fun to be made a fool of, especially when you have already endured so much.

I was that person. I was that person who left my spiritual and cultural identity, my internal compass, at the door so I could fit in. So in moments when I should have shown up like this woman in Mark 14, as a priest, or as the Syrophoenician woman as a truth teller, or as the Samaritan Woman as a community organizer, or as the women at the tomb as a healer and ritual keeper—I hid, allowing someone else to do the work God had given me to do a long time ago so that I did not take up too much space or so my work wasn't exploited for someone else's gain. I shrunk myself to fit into a box of someone else's expectations so that I could be found palatable, pleasing, and agreeable instead of the angry Black woman or Jezebel/Sapphire stereotype or all the other tropes that people use to define/characterize Black womanhood to keep us in our place. I kept seeking permission for things that God had already placed in my heart until I realized I did not need permission to be used and called by God, to use my experience as a Black woman to hold systems—and sometimes people—accountable for the ways in which they perpetuate white supremacy and patriarchy and dishonor the name of God.

I got to a point in life where the boxes, like most of the pants I own, no longer fit. And so you know what I started doing? I started looking for historical and familial examples of where Black women like myself, in spite of what they faced, got *ovah*. Persevered. Pulled through and made it to the other side. I looked at the writings of Black women in texts like *My Soul is a Witness*, edited by Gloria Wade Gayles.

One essay sticks out to me in this collection particularly, by Bernice Johnson Reagon, and her piece, "Sing Oh Barren One." Johnson, an activist, songwriter, and founder of Sweet Honey in the Rock, reflects back on how a friend of hers asked her to write a song based on Isaiah 54.1–10 for her ordination. Though Johnson initially struggled with the text, displeased and disgusted with the anger that God displayed towards Israel, she came to understand how Isaiah speaks to "our resistance to be the leading voice of the time" (2001, p. 138). Johnson encourages us, affirming that, in spite of how we may be viewed by the society that we live in, we have an obligation to lift our voices to sing and share the wisdom that the Holy Spirit has placed in our hearts.

I can't count the number of times I have gone back to this piece over the years, each reading accompanied with new pen marks as something about the story strikes me differently. As a matter of fact, the book as a whole—now covered in multicolored post-it notes with my scribblings throughout—reminds me of who I am and how God is operating within me, in spite of how I might feel, in spite of what others might say. This work helps me see how we as a people have pulled through, how we have overcome, and I would be remiss if I didn't take the teachings that they offer and apply them to my own life.

And of course, there are so many other (re)memberings, so many other readings, so many other Black women, including my mother, so many other examples of how folks have moved forward. My mother doesn't have a really good singing voice, but I remember the Saturday mornings and drives to school, when she would turn the radio up, blasting Yolanda Adams, singing and praying and calling on God for help when she had reached her breaking point. And I saw God meet her and answer her; those (re)memberings encourage me in my own faith journey after all of these years.

And I wonder, I wonder if this was Roxanne; if she had finally reached her breaking point and was ready to dive right in no matter what it cost. Maybe she had been waiting at the back of the synagogue all of her life, from the first time she heard the whisper of the Spirit when she was a little girl. Maybe she was hanging around house churches week after week, hoping that someone could see the light, the anointing that was on her fingertips. All she needed was a chance. All she needed was a moment to prove to the world that God spoke through messy women too! And maybe like me, she was nearing forty and realized that if she did not break free and walk forward in her own convictions, she was never going to fully realize her calling.

"Truly I tell you, wherever the good news is proclaimed in the whole world, what she has done will be told in remembrance of her" (Mark 14.9, NRSV). Go back and get Roxanne's story. But go back and get your own, too! Remember your call. Remember your experience. Bring to mind the history of our people, study and ruminate on how we made it over religiously. We can do this through ritual and ceremony, something that the liturgical calendar provides. Or by memorializing events of significance such as the murder of George Floyd, Juneteenth, the 400th commemoration. We remember through testimony—"but they conquered him by the blood of the lamb and the word of their testimony" (Revelations 12.11, NRSV)—which is why testimony service is so important to us as it provides a collective reminder of how we have come this far by faith. We study the Word and study the texts that have meant cultural significance to our people. And we commit to not forget again, understanding that forgetting serves no one but ciswhitesupremacistheteropatriarchy. We must understand, in the spirit of Sankofa, that if we want to move forward, we have to continuously look back.

Study Guide

This study guide is designed to deepen the reading experience of the person(s) holding this book and to encourage one's own writing process. Grab a journal or use the last few pages of this book to engage in this exercise. Consider preparing your writing space by opening with prayer and/or meditation, turning on soft music, and burning incense. Make yourself a cup of tea. Get your favorite pen. Now write.

Questions for Part One: Incomplete Stories

- When you reflect on *Incomplete Stories*, what pieces resonate with you in regard to understanding your cultural and familial history?
- How has (re)membering caused you pain? Where has (re)membering brought you joy?
- What stories about your past are you in the process of (re)covering to find liberation and greater understanding?

Questions for Part Two: A Black Woman's Journey of (Re)Membrance

- What journeys have you taken that have helped you (re)member?
- If you journal, look back over some of your previous journal entries. What do these entries tell you about the person you once were, who you are now, or where you might be headed? If you do not journal,

consider integrating the discipline into your daily routine.

Questions for Part Three: Go Back and Get It!

- How do you identify with Roxanne's story? When have you been silenced and ignored when you otherwise had something to offer from your vast gifts and insight?
- What things have seduced you into forgetting the promises that God has already spoken over you? What steps can you take to (re)cover those memories and walk in your calling?

Your Story

Your Story

Your Story

Your Story

Your Story

Your Story

References

Adedayo, E. (2020). *The Gospel According to a Black Woman.* Aya Media Publishing, LLC.

Akbar, N. (1998). *Know thy self.* Productions & Associates, Inc

Anzaldua, G. (1987). *Borderlands/La frontera: The new mestizo.* Spinsters/Aunt Lute.

Atta, D.T. (2018). Calling on the Divine and sacred energy of queens: Bringing Afrikan indigenous women and spirituality into the academy. In Perlow, O.N., Wheeler, D.I., Bethea, S.L., Scott, B.M. (Eds). *Black women's liberatory pedagogies: Resistance, transformation, and healing within and beyond the academy, p. 227–244.* Palgrave MacMillan.

Bethea, S.L. (2018). Kuja nyumbani (coming home): Using African-Centered pedagogy to educate Black students in the academy. In Perlow, O.N., Wheeler, D.I., Bethea, S.L., Scott, B.M. (Eds). *Black women's liberatory pedagogies: Resistance, transformation, and healing within and beyond the academy* (p. 295–320). Palgrave MacMillan.

Blackburn Center (2020, February 26). *Black women and domestic violence.* Retrieved May 5, 2021 from https://www.blackburncenter.org/post/2020/02/26/black-women-domestic-violence

Cannon, K.G. (1995). Surviving the blight. In Wade-Gayles, G. (ed). *My soul is a witness: African American women's spirituality, p. 19 – 26.* Beacon Press

Coates, T. (2015). *Between the world and me.* Spiegel and Grau

Dillard, C.B. (2012). *Learning to (re)member the things we've learned to forget.* Peter Lang

Dillard, C (2016). Turning the ships around: A case study of (re)membering as transnational endarkened feminist inquiry and praxis for Black teachers, *Educational Studies, 52*(5), 406-423, DOI: 10.1080/00131946.2016.1214916.

Dixon, C. (2009, October 26). The opposite of truth is forgetting: An interview with Roxanne Dunbar-Ortiz. *Upping the Anti,* Retrieved November 11, 2020 from https://uppingtheanti.org/journal/uta/number-six

Fanon, F (1967). *Black skins, white masks.* Grove Press, Inc

Giddings, P. (1984). *When and where I enter.* Perennial.

hooks, b. (1994/2007). *Teaching to transgress: Education as the practice of freedom.* Routledge

Jackson, F.M. (1995). "In the morning when I rise": My hands in spiritual soil. In Wade-Gayles, G. (ed). *My soul is a witness: African American women's spirituality, p 48–54.* Beacon Press

Jimenez, R.M. (2020). Community cultural wealth pedagogies: Cultivating autoethnographic counternarratives and migration capital. *American Education Research Journal, 57*(2), 775-807. DOI: 10.3102/0002831219866148

Lorde, A. (1984/2017). *Sister outsider*. Crossing Press.

mcfadden, s. (2017, August 2). White Milwaukee lied to itself for decades, and in 1967 the truth came out. *Timeline*. Retrieved August 2017 from https://timeline.com/milwaukee-long-hot-summer-252057567975

Menakem, R. (2017). *My grandmother's hands. Racialized trauma and the pathway to mending our hearts and bodies.* Central Recovery Press

Milner, H. R. (2007). Race, narrative inquiry, and self-study in curriculum and teacher education. *Education and Urban Society, 39*(4), 584-609. DOI:10.1177/0013124507301577

Patterson, O. (2018). *Slavery and social death: A comparative study.* Harvard University Press

Ransby, B. (2018). *Making all Black lives matter: Reimagining freedom in the 21st century*. University of California

Reagon, B.J. (1995). "Sing oh barren one". In Wade-Gayles, G. (ed). *My soul is a witness: African American women's spirituality, p.137–143*. Boston, MA: Beacon Press

Sharpe, C. (2016). *In the wake: On Blackness and being.* Duke University Press.

Terborg-Penn, R. (2001). The Spirit keeps the memory of the ancestors alive. In Wade-Gayles, G. (ed). *My soul is a witness: African American women's spirituality, p 65–70*. Beacon Press.

Tolliver, D. (2015). Africentrism: Standing on its own cultural ground. *Wiley Periodicals (147)* 59 - 70, DOI: 10.1002/ace.20142

Walker, A. (1983). *In search of our mother's gardens.* Harcourt Brace & Company

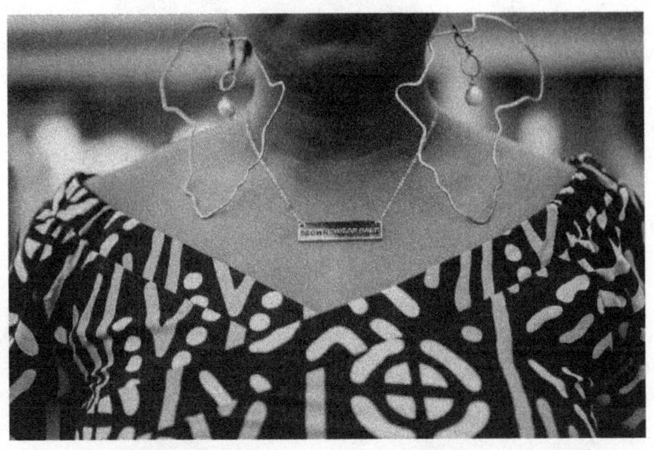

To find out more about Ebony Adedayo visit
https://ayacollectivemn.com.

or

IG: ebonyadedayo

Other books by Ebony Adedayo:

The Gospel According to a Black Woman
(Released November 2020)

Embracing a Holistic Faith: Essays on Biblical Justice
(Released April 2014)